D1214615

PAINTING
THE SOUTHWEST LANDSCAPE
IN WATERCOLOR

THE WINDMILL
Courtesy Mrs. R. A. Drum

PAINTING
THE SOUTHWEST LANDSCAPE
IN WATERCOLOR

GERRY PEIRCE

REINHOLD PUBLISHING CORPORATION / *New York*

This Book Is Dedicated to My Students Who
Have All Helped to Make a Difficult
Instructor a Better Watercolorist.

DESIGNED BY MYRON HALL III

TYPE SET AND PRINTED BY THE COMET PRESS, INC.

BOUND BY RUSSELL-RUTTER COMPANY, INC.

FOREWORD

Through this Foreword, the many devoted watercolor students of Gerry Peirce express their gratitude for this long-awaited book. It is more than a manual of his orderly course in the techniques and fundamental how-to-paint procedures of this elusive medium. Beyond the necessary routines on materials and their handling, here are many of the philosophies of composition, design—and life in general—that have made Gerry a uniquely inspiring teacher.

Many of us who now welcome this handbook have been variously exposed to earlier art training before studying watercolor with Gerry Peirce. "The business value of beauty" has been a constant factor in the creative phases of printing and publishing for this writer. The adventures of collecting have stirred others to express their creative impulses by painting in watercolor. Art teachers come to Gerry to become better teachers. And the intellectual stimulus of this contact is quite as rewarding to all of us as the discovery by many beginners that they can really "paint a picture."

It is appropriate to this cherished teacher-student relationship that members of Gerry's group have financed the Tucson Watercolor Guild, building ample studios that survey the Arizona desert and the nearby mountains. They have provided for continuity with a sound endowment that insures for men and women in these strenuous times the cosmic relief of creative work in the arts.

Said Eliot O'Hara in 1946: "As a contribution to the country's store of culture and advancement in the arts, one good school could outweigh two museums." From such a school comes this demonstration that these orderly, systematic procedures for watercolor painting have been enriched in Gerry's teaching by the approach to art and to living which has endeared him to so many of his disciples.

Harry Gage

Preparing for creative work in printing and publishing, Harry Gage studied at the Art Institute of Chicago (1905-09), receiving a European scholarship. During some forty years of business activity (and "Sunday painting"), he became president of the American Institute of Graphic Arts (1932-34) and treasurer of the American Federation of Arts (1943-44). On retiring from business he began his studies with Gerry Peirce in 1952. He is now an active member of North Shore Arts Association in Gloucester, Massachusetts, also of the Copley Society of Boston, and an associate member of Rockport Art Association.

I wish to thank Charles and Hazel Archer of Tucson
for their excellent photography which has contributed
so greatly to the artistic and educational value
of this book, Margo Adams for her helpful suggestions
and stenographic assistance, and all those who have
so graciously loaned paintings from their private
collections. I am especially grateful to Raymond
Burr for his able assistance in securing the color
transparencies. My deepest gratitude, however, rests
with Priscilla, my wife, for without her encouragement
and perseverance, this book would have remained unwritten.

Gerry Peirce

Color Illustrations

CONTENTS

YUCCAS
Courtesy Louise L. Serpa

INTRODUCTION

This book is written for those who like watercolor—whether they be mature painters, beginning students, or Sunday painters. The first few chapters deal with the craft of painting, the brush, water, paper and pigment, value, hue and intensity, field equipment and light. They probe into such basic problems as composition, glazes, and the three planes of landscape.

The craft of painting is one thing, but creative painting is another. Creative painting is not apart from craft but transcends it and is the ultimate goal of all serious painters. And so throughout the book, interwoven with this basic instruction, moves a theme that deals with the more intangible aspects of creative painting. For to the knowledge of one's craft and the mastery of technical skill must be added a high degree of awareness and feeling before any emotion of creative significance can be expressed. The final chapters are devoted to expression and perception.

It is my hope that these chapters will be for you as doors set ajar. May you find something new, interesting, and creatively exciting as you swing the pages open and enter.

Chapter 1

BRUSH, WATER,

PIGMENT AND PAPER

The Brush

Let us start with the idea that watercolor should look like watercolor, reflecting the qualities that are characteristic of the medium. This requires the proper tools—brush, paper, water, and pigment. First, we must select a suitable brush—one that carries plenty of water, and gets over the paper rapidly when necessary, and is useful for a variety of rough brush strokes and lines. A 1-inch flat red sable or sabeline brush fills the bill adequately. Since most of our painting will be done with this brush, we should know its various parts and their specific uses.

A brush is composed of a handle, ferrule and hairs (Figure 1). It has a balance point. The forward end of the brush hairs is called the edge, sometimes the chisel edge, to distinguish it from the side. As the hairs taper back from the edge, they form the shoulder. The body or flat of the brush lies between the shoulder and the ferrule. The end of the tapering wood handle is the point. The edge of the brush is used for graded washes, edge lines, thin lines and some dry brush strokes, and the shoulder for a variety of rough brush strokes. The body or flat of the brush creates even broader rough textures. The side is used for wide lines and narrow rough brush strokes and the point for making dark lines.

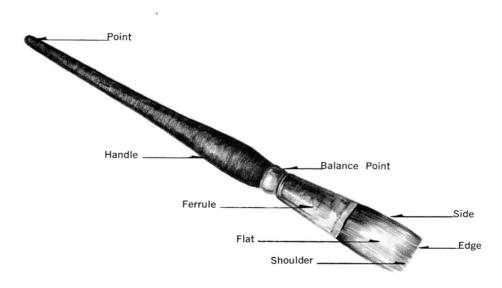

FIGURE 1. KNOW THE PARTS OF YOUR BRUSH.

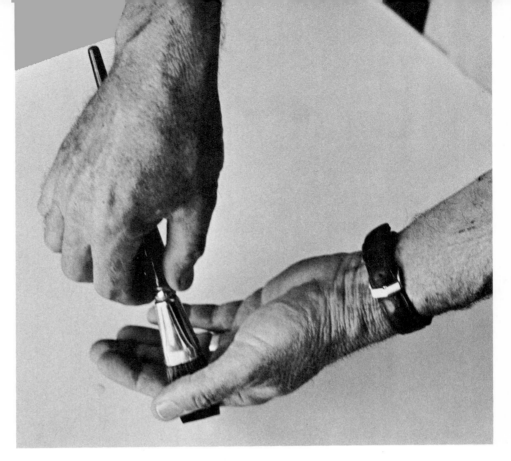

FIGURE 2. SAMPLING THE BRUSH.

We have described the brush physically. How much of our feeling or sensitivity can we expect it to be capable of translating? We have already claimed a great deal for it. Preparing it to do its job at the right time and place is one of the most important factors in watercolor painting. This is not something that can be completely thought out. It is here that one's feeling nature must somehow step in and assist, so that one is either aware that the brush is set to do the job, or that it is not. For myself, there is no better way of achieving this feeling control over a brush than slicking the hairs out between the index finger and thumb of the left hand (Figure 2), or if the brush does not need to be shaped, touching the edge to the base of the thumb to feel how wet it is (Figure 3). If I sense that the brush is too wet or too dry, has too little or too much pigment, I go back to the water pail and start over. The brush is washed thoroughly, then sampled between the fingers as before. The unnecessary water is pressed out and the brush is tested against the thumb. Sometimes only the corner of the edge touches the water, allowing but a small amount to pull through the hairs by capillary attraction. It is again sampled between the fingers and, if all is well, pigment is picked up and pulled out on the palette. The brush is evenly loaded and then shaped between thumb and index finger. This process may be gone through several times before the brush ever touches paper. A paint rag tucked in the belt is used to keep the left hand dry and sensitive. Remember that the brush can be dried in two ways—by pressing water out and by adding pigment. These are subtleties that will be better understood after the student actually begins his experiments with the brush. With added experience we discover that muscular coordination has a lot to do with it. This is more difficult psychologically than anything else, for in this age we are much

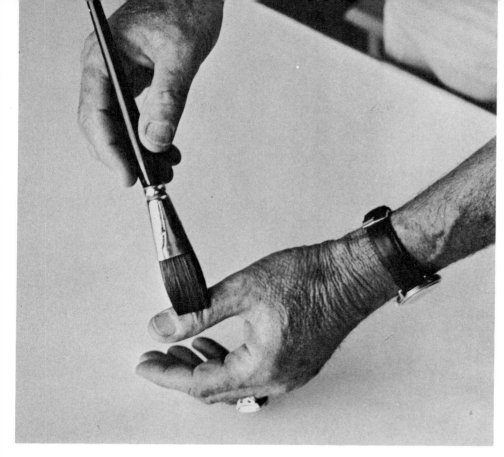

FIGURE 3. TESTING THE BRUSH.

more concerned with the product than with what produces it. We quite naturally follow this pattern of conditioning when we begin to experiment with brush strokes and washes. If we get a few interesting textures, we marvel at what we have done and give little or no thought to how we did it. What part of our muscular structure was used, the fingers, wrist, forearm, shoulders or the whole body? Various strokes are done with different muscles. If we are aware of the muscles used when we achieve an interesting brush stroke or a texture that we like, the experiment with our brushes will really pay off.

Water

Watercolors are at their best when they are wet, for when they dry, the color loses some of its brilliance and the values lighten. It is important, however, that a painting reflect the quality which says, "This was done with water," even though the water has long since evaporated.

Some painters use nothing but distilled water, though this is an extravagance for most watercolorists. Good tap water if not excessively hard will do. The most important thing is to use plenty of it. For inside work, a large pailful is none too much. In the field this may not be possible, but use as large a container as you can and always carry extra water with you. Remember that water should be used with the greatest abandon. When working inside, assume that copious quantities are going on the floor. If the floor is not the kind that will be enhanced by the beauty of a watercolor patina, put down papers and a drop cloth. If you are unduly concerned about the floor, your watercolors will probably die of thirst.

When applying water to the paper prior to adding pigment, use more water than is needed. When the paper is amply covered and the water evenly distributed with the brush, hold it to the light and see if it glints all over the surface. If it does, the paper is uniformly wet. If there is too much water, it can be dried with the brush. Pigment can also be lifted from the paper with a brush at the moment the shine goes off the paper. In both instances, however, the brush must be drier than the paper. A hard or distinct edge cannot be painted in water color unless the painting surface is perfectly dry. Touch the paper with the outer side of the little finger. If it feels cool, it is not completely dry, for evaporation is still taking place. Fusing or painting into a wet surface is a matter of timing in relation to the wetness or dryness of the paper and the amount of water and pigment in the brush. Balloons are made (intentionally or unintentionally) by applying a wet brush to a semi-dry area. If this is intentional, it still is a matter of timing.

Pigments

Color is light, and pigment is the artist's equivalent for color. Pigment quality in watercolor is actually light quality. To reflect luminosity and clarity in a painting requires an understanding of pigments and when and where to use them. Although there are many theories and rules about color, there is probably nothing in the realm of painting to which theories and rules are less applicable. We use color by feeling, not by rule. We can only feel the rightness of colors together.

As you become more and more aware of color relationships, you will find that the color of a flower is related quite astonishingly to its leaves, and that when the blossom is placed against another green, it is not quite as perfect. You will begin to see the little animals of the earth and feel the perfect harmony of their color in relation to the soil in which they live. This is true in all of nature, the birds in the air, the mountains in the mist and in bright sun, the stones on the desert. As you feel this harmony and unity in nature, your awareness will reflect in your painting.

As we go on in this book and begin work with a full palette, our pigments and their uses will be carefully explained. However, for experiments with a graded wash and various brush strokes, we will limit ourselves to black. Two kinds of black are commonly used in watercolor, ivory and lamp. Ivory is a warm black, lamp is cool. Both are precipitating pigments, that is, composed of granules bound together with an adhesive which causes the particles to adhere to the paper. In student grade pigment, the granule is often coarsely ground and when a wash is put on, is apt to settle in the depressions in the paper, creating a texture which the English call "puddling out." When fresh pigment is put out, it is often difficult to handle because of its softness. Care should be taken in stroking it out on the palette, completely mixing it with the water in the brush and filling the brush evenly, to avoid unfortunate blobs.

Ivory black is made from carbon derived from burned bones, and lamp black is made from soot. Both are impervious to light and both will wash off the paper fairly easily.

Paper

Watercolors should look as though they were painted on paper for this is one of the most characteristic features of the medium. Not only is white paper the light source of a painting, and the source of luminosity, but even the small unpainted white paper areas add sparkle and quality. Watercolor papers run the full gamut from rough to smooth, from soft to hard, from handmade to machine-made. The surface of a good rough watercolor paper is a series of elevations and depressions, and highly magnified in cross section, might look like the illustration shown in Figure 4. How the depressions are flooded with water and the elevations are touched with pigment is of paramount interest to the watercolorist.

The brush, water and pigment are constants in watercolor painting. Paper is not a constant unless we make it so. A watercolor painted on hard paper is apt to be more brilliant than one on soft paper, and our brush, water and pigment produce quite a different result on smooth paper than they do on rough. When one is trying to master the technique of watercolor painting it is a good idea to stay with one paper, for then all four factors are kept constant. For practice purposes, a good machine-made paper with a medium rough surface, and as white as possible will serve. It should be about 140-pound weight and as similar to handmade paper of that weight as can be found. If the paper is clipped to a board, it should dry flat after washes are applied, though stretching paper is much better even for practice purposes.

Can one become aware in relation to paper? I believe that it is most expedient to develop a sensitivity along this line. Examine a piece of watercolor paper carefully before buying it. Feel it, look it over for scars, dents and scratches, and hold it against the light to see if it has any dark spots in it. All handmade papers seem to

FIGURE 4. ELEVATIONS AND DEPRESSIONS IN ROUGH WATERCOLOR PAPER.

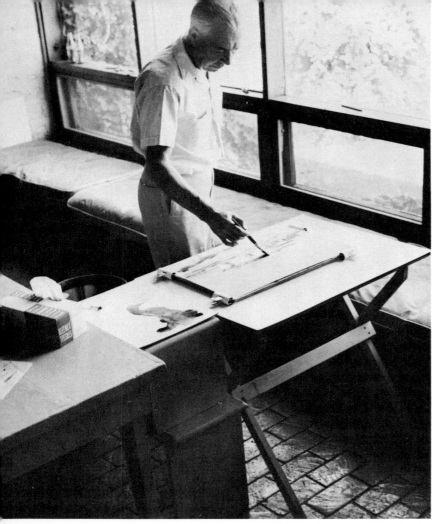

FIGURE 5. A CONVENIENT WORKING ARRANGEMENT.

FIGURE 6. TOOLS SHOULD BE CLOSE AT HAND.

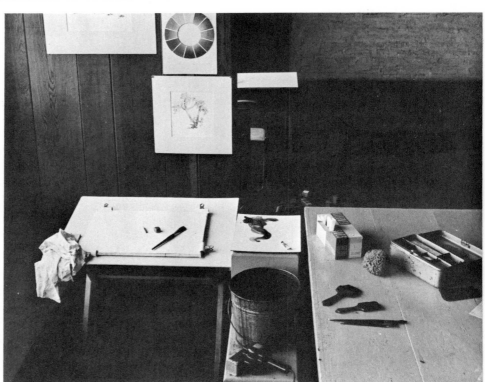

have a slight coating over the surface. If this is light, it will wash off easily. If it is heavy the paper must be carefully washed with cold water and a sponge or it will be practically waterproof. This coating cannot be seen but it can be felt.

When beginning a painting, be careful to select a paper well adapted to your subject. Handmade papers, even of the same make and weight vary considerably, one being a trifle rougher or harder than another. These variables are discernible only through the sense of touch. Gently snap the corner of a piece of paper to determine its hardness. Hard papers make a crisper sound than soft ones. What I feel about a piece of paper will make a great deal of difference when I begin painting. Do not be disturbed if you are not at first sensitive to these differences; with experience they will become obvious.

Studio Order

Every artist should plan his studio working area in a way best suited to his own convenience. Figure 5 shows the basic design of my working space, which is arranged in a manner to create order and convenience for me.

The painting table is 30 by 24 by 30 inches and has a top which tips easily to an angle of about 10 degrees. It is covered with white Formica which is easy to keep clean and makes a good hard surface for both drawing and painting. The light comes from a north window to the left. In front of the table is a wall suitable for tacking up sketches, and also a color wheel (Figure 6). On the wall behind the table is a mirror for checking drawings and compositions. When a drawing or painting in any stage is seen in reverse, its imperfections are easy to perceive. I think of my studio mirror as a quiet but efficient instructor and critic.

On the end of a bench to the right of the table is an open box; the top is level with the table and holds my studio palette. The box has a shelf for pencils, erasers, extra brushes, etc. that might otherwise clutter my table. The palette is 12 by 16 inches and is also made of white Formica. Before I use it I scour it lightly with a kitchen cleanser to prevent water and pigment from pooling. The paper is clipped to a piece of Upsom board 15½ by 20 inches with No. 4 Hunt clips. These have been painted white as I find they are much less distracting against the paper than if they had been left black. Since the paper expands and contracts during stages of painting, the clips have to be moved somewhat to freely permit this action. The water pail is next to the palette on the bench, and a little to the right to avoid any hazard of dripping water on the paper. Since it is always in the same place, it is not necessary to even look toward it. The long table affords me plenty of room for anything I might need when I am working, though I try not to have too much out. It is unnecessary to create confusion simply because one has room to do so. The hair drier, next to the pail, is certainly not a necessity, but when the weather is heavy and washes take too long to dry, it is a luxury one can ill afford to be without. And last, though of paramount importance, are the H.B. pencils. Mine are cut in thirds so that they can be held inside the hand when drawing, thus avoiding finger action. Harder pencils will dent the paper and leave dark lines after the pigment is applied. Softer pencils will not erase. On a good handmade paper, art gum will remove H.B. pencil lines from the painting after it is finished. The paint rag is tucked in my belt when work begins, instantly available for use. It is never held in the left hand.

Hand and Brush

There are two basic brush positions; one vertical (Figure 7), the other horizontal (Figure 8). The brush is held in the vertical position to utilize the edge in executing graded washes, edge lines, thin lines and some rough brushing. Note the position of the index finger in relation to the point of the brush, and of the little finger near the center of the handle. The edge of the brush barely touches the paper. The horizontal position (Figure 8) is used for rough brush strokes either with the shoulder or flat of the brush.

Put the brush on the table and pick it up at the balance point between the index finger and thumb. Do not allow the fingers to go under the brush. There are two ways of changing the angle, one by rolling the hand and forearm, the other by tipping the brush with the two middle fingers or with the little finger under the brush. Try moving the brush from the horizontal to the vertical position and then back again without putting it down. Practice this until it is an easy flowing movement and the brush and hand seem to belong together. Note as you do this what your fingers, wrist and arm are doing.

When using the side of the brush for wide lines or narrow rough brush strokes, it is held sideways in the horizontal position. Index finger and thumb are at the balance point.

FIGURE 7. VERTICAL POSITION.

FIGURE 8. HORIZONTAL POSITION.

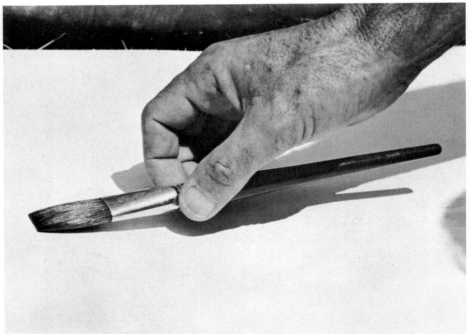

18

FALLEN TREE
Courtesy Doris Fletcher

19

Experiments with the Edge of the Brush—Graded Wash

With our painting materials set up as shown in Figure 5, let us try some experiments with the brush and see how various kinds of brush strokes are done. However, remember that there is no basic how-to-do-it method outside of your own awareness of what brings about a satisfactory result, or your inner feeling of improper coordination when the result is not satisfactory.

In most watercolors the largest areas are executed in graded washes, evenly graduated from light to dark or vice versa. Washes can be done in a number of ways. We will paint this one from light to dark on dry paper. Graded washes are done with the edge of the brush which is held in a vertical position (Figure 9). The attempt is to flood the indentations in the paper evenly.

With the H.B. pencil draw a straight line across the paper near the top. In the photograph the line is shown darker than normal for the sake of clarity (Figure 9). Tip the paper or table top at an angle of about 10 degrees so that the water will run toward you. Fill the brush with water and apply at the base of the pencil line. Hold the brush lightly and in an almost vertical position, the edge just touching as it travels back and forth across the paper. Do not press down as this cuts off the flow of water. Too great an angle of the brush reduces the force of gravity and produces rough brushing. One should stand straight, reaching out rather than bending over. Keep the elbow relaxed but not bent. Stand back from the table, feet slightly apart. Use a free, easy arm movement. The wrist and lower arm turn slightly to change the angle of the brush. The shoulders swing a bit and the weight of the body shifts a little from the left foot to the right. The whole body is used in this stroke and the paper is thought of as continuing a foot or so beyond its edge. The stroke is done as though one were carrying through a golf shot. There is no hurry. It is the feeling of coordination that counts. Carry the water down about 3 inches below the pencil line. Dry the brush slightly between the fingers and pull out a small amount of pigment on the palette. Mix well and charge the brush evenly and deeply into the hairs. A light value is all that is necessary.

You will note that a bead of water has collected at the dry edge of the paper. To this bead add the pigment in the brush in the same way that you applied the water. The brush is carried half in the bead of water and half in the dry area so that only part of it is painted. Go back to the palette and pull out more pigment, a little darker this time, and add it to the bead which has collected again. Continue to the bottom of the sheet in the same manner, graduating the color until the end of the wash is about middle value. Move the clips as you go. Do not work back into the wash as this will only produce a picky, messy result. When the wash is finished, level the paper and dry the brush thoroughly, pressing it out in the paint rag. Pick up the water at the edge of the paper to keep it from pulling back into the wash and forming balloons. Remove the clips and dry them. You will be surprised to see how much lighter the wash is when it is dry.

The graded wash on dry paper calls for proper brush control, coordination of the whole body, a feeling for the right amount of water and pigment in the brush, and plenty of practice.

FIGURE 9. A GRADED WASH.

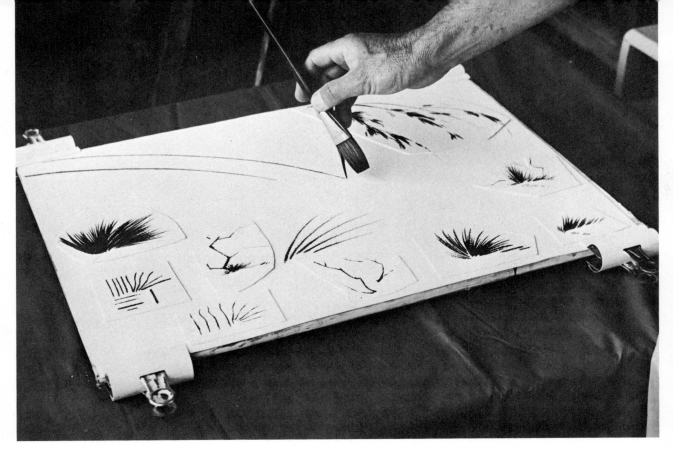

FIGURE 10. EDGE LINES AND FINE LINES. (Examples are cutouts except at top left and center.)

Edge Lines

A straight or curved line made by the chisel edge calls for careful shaping of the brush while it is semi-dry. Holding it in a vertical position, exert a slight pressure downward from the shoulder until the edge just touches the paper as shown in Figure 10. Be careful not to bend the edge. To curve the line, the brush handle is rolled slightly with the fore part of the thumb.

A brush edge may be set in a curve between the fingers. This curve repeated on paper a number of times is a convenient way of indicating the characteristic growth of a bush or tree. An edge line may be elongated by putting the closer corner of the brush on the paper first, pushing forward and stretching the hairs as the edge is pressed down.

Fine Lines

It is often more convenient to make a fine line in pigment with the brush you are using than to reach for a small pointed brush to make the line. To practice this stroke, charge the brush deeply with water and pigment. Then pull a small group of hairs away from the rest of the brush, or separate them with a knife blade. The brush should be held sideways, between the thumb and first finger, at the balancing point, the little finger on the ferrule and the index finger on the handle. As the line is made, tip the brush toward you or in the opposite direction from which the line is going, as in the illustration (Figure 10). This will keep the hairs from pressing back into the mass. Long, thin lines are made by keeping the arm fairly stiff and swinging the shoulders. It is a body stroke. Shorter lines are made by turning the wrist.

Some Rough Brush Strokes

In the rough-brush stroke, pigment is applied to the elevations of the paper without flooding the depressions. These strokes are the descriptive adjectives of watercolor and they can be done in a variety of ways.

Most rough-brush strokes are made with the brush in a horizontal position, though a few are executed with the brush held in a vertical position. There are three factors that determine the nature of the rough-brush stroke. First, the angle at which the brush is held. Second, the speed at which it travels. Third, the amount of water in the brush. If the brush is held in a vertical position, it must either be quite dry or else move very rapidly; otherwise the depressions in the paper will be flooded.

Shape a semi-dry brush to a chisel edge. Holding it in a vertical position, place a horizontal edge line on the paper but do not lift the brush (Figure 11). Contract the thumb, index finger and middle finger until the wrist feels tight but not rigid. With a quick lifting snap of the fingers, the brush is moved forward and upward. This is completely a finger stroke. Many varieties of this stroke are possible as the edge line is placed in different directions. I use it frequently in reducing palm trees to a common denominator. If the brush holds more water and is held at a slight angle, frayed banana leaves are simply and easily symbolized. This stroke is sometimes called a flip stroke.

FIGURE 11. VERTICAL ROUGH BRUSHING. (Examples of strokes are cutouts.)

Experiments with the Shoulder of the Brush—Rough Brushing

If a brush is a good water carrier, it will thicken in the middle when the hairs are saturated. This creates a long, full shoulder adaptable for rough brushing. A long-haired, thick brush is a better water carrier and more suited to rough brushing than a thin one. A short-haired brush is not good for either purpose; if the brush is thin, the shoulder is too flat; if the brush is thick, the shoulder is too sharp. At best, a short-haired brush does not have a good water-carrying capacity.

Fill your brush with water and shape it. Holding it in the horizontal position, place it on the paper as though you were going to begin a rough brush stroke. As this is done, lift the brush slightly so that the shoulder will ride flat on the paper. There is a slight pressure downward. Lift the brush and examine it. You will see that the underside is spoon shaped and the shoulder is longer than when the hairs were straight. The more pressure used, the more curved the shoulder becomes.

Charge the brush with more water than pigment, and shape until it is semi-dry, making sure that the body is permeated with pigment, not just the tip, and that there are no blobs of paint. Starting at the left side of the paper, move the brush in a straight line to the right side without changing the angle. Think of the paper as extending beyond its limits and try not to lift the brush in an upward sweep as you come to the right edge. The stroke is done from the shoulder, elbow slightly bent. The whole body sways a little as one's weight shifts from the left foot to the right. To steady the hand, let the little finger ride on the paper.

An experimental stroke begins with the brush held flat. As it is moved to the right, it rough-brushes. Do this for about 3 inches. Without lifting the brush, increase the angle to about 80 degrees and move it along the paper for another 3 inches. This will produce a graded wash. The brush indications in the upper part of Figure 12 were made in this way. Alternate these two brush strokes until you have crossed the paper, first the brush held almost flat or at an angle of about 10 degrees for rough brushing, then lifted to 80 degrees for the wash.

For a vertical rough brush stroke, turn the brush so that the handle is toward you, the edge away. This is a push stroke starting from a horizontal line and pushing up in a scoop-like motion. This is shown by the hand in Figure 12. The edge of the brush is not disturbed. The shoulder hairs do the work. This is done from the shoulder, elbow firm but slightly bent, and is a quick muscular action of the shoulder and chest muscles.

Try all these rough brush strokes, changing the water and pigment content in the brush, changing the angle of the brush, increasing and decreasing the speed. No matter what kind of brush texture you make, try to be conscious or aware of how it is done, and how your hand and body are coordinated.

Experiments with the Flat of the Brush—Wide Textural Strokes

When the shoulder of the brush is in operation, its angle varies. When the flat is used, it is held in a uniformly horizontal position, fingers riding on the paper. As the brush is turned and rotated, the handle swings in arcs. The action is mainly in the wrist and forearm with now and then a little shoulder action. The edge of the brush is not disturbed, only the under hairs of the flat of the brush. Textural strokes made with this part of the brush are generally broad and are often used for foliage.

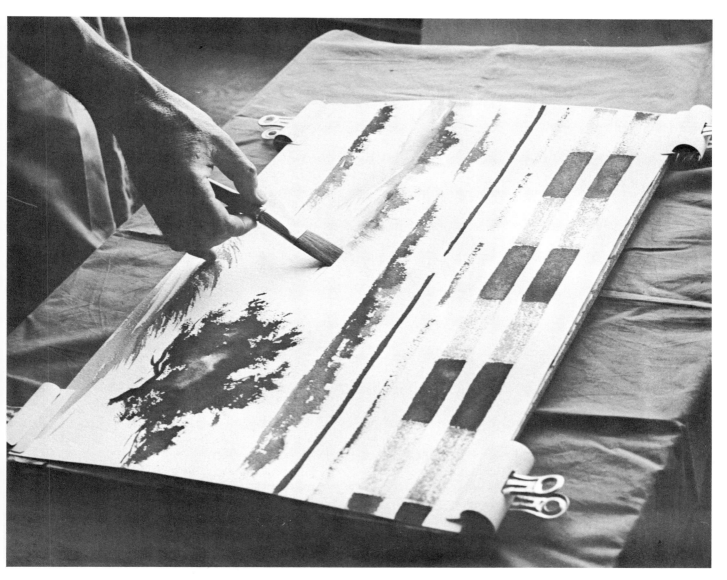

FIGURE 12. VARIOUS ROUGH BRUSH STROKES.

Experiments with the Side of the Brush—
Wide Lines—Narrow Rough Brushing

When the brush is held on its side in the horizontal position, it will make either broad lines or narrow rough brush strokes. This is dependent, of course, on angle, speed and moisture. Vertical rough brushing is also made with the side of the brush by using a quick finger-and-wrist movement upward, similar to the push stroke.

Experiments with the Point of the Brush—Dark Lines

The wood point of the 1-inch brush, the end of the handle, is used for making fine dark lines. These are put in when the paper is wet. The indentation, made by the point in the paper, fills with pigment and, as the paper dries, the line darkens.

The preceding explanation of the various ways of holding and moving our brushes to produce some specific desired results are right for my hands. They may not be right for yours. For your hands, they are only generalized principles.

With these principles in mind—begin!

Questions and Answers.

Q. Does watercolor always dry lighter?

A. Yes. Lighter values dry several degrees lighter than darker ones do. Some pigments dry lighter than others.

Q. Why put on more water than is needed?

A. It is always better to begin with a constant which is established by a uniformly wet area. Variety can then be achieved when it is desired by drying portions of the area with the brush. The practice of putting on a small amount of water and distributing it is such a slow process that generally the first part of the area is dry by the time the last part is moistened.

Q. Do you use a ruler to draw?

A. No. My drawn line may not be too interesting but I feel there is nothing less interesting than a ruled line.

Q. Why isn't charcoal good to draw with?

A. It is. I frequently use it, especially if the painting is to be dark and of low intensity. The charcoal then combines well with the pigment. If the painting is to be light and high in intensity, I use a pencil because charcoal would lower the brilliance of the pigment.

Q. Do you use Kleenex on the painting?

A. Occasionally, to lighten areas and for certain textures. I use it continually for cleaning and drying my palette.

Q. How do you tip the paper at 10 degrees without holding on to it?

A. Try a couple of penny match boxes or something about that size.

Q. I don't see why I have to be aware when I paint.

A. You don't. You may paint better and enjoy it more if you are.

Q. Why should watercolors look like watercolors?

A. I feel that the reason for asking this question is more significant than the question. Many believe that the reality of a painting does not lie in the way it is done but in its emotional and expressive quality. This is true. This truth, however, is not a license for technical inability or indifference. Painting is a language existing for the purpose of expressing ideas, emotions and experiences that could not be expressed in any other way. There is also a rightness to all things. We do not expect a lecturer to deviate from the English language and hold forth for half an hour in Chinese. We expect boys to be boys and girls to be girls. We expect apples to grow from apple trees and elephants to bring forth elephants, not kangaroos. The integrity of the medium should be maintained. Then a rightness in relation to expression, plus an integrated quality of beauty, is established.

Chapter 2

FURTHER

EXPERIMENTS

There is probably no place in the world as tranquil as the desert in late afternoon. Although it may be more pleasant in the fall, winter and spring than in mid-summer, the desert always has its own inimitable mystery and charm. Clouds drift gently across the sky, whispering misleading promises of rain. Mist rises from the slopes of the serene mountains, and dust devils lazily swirl in the dry washes. The distant trees merge into the hills and a fleck of sun brightens an open sandy area. Nearby are the bushes and plants that have learned to live in this land of little rain—the creosote,

prickly pear, yucca and saguaro. There are the tawny grasses, the franseria and the burro weed. Quail call back and forth and the doves speak in pearl-like tones. The jack rabbits are moving, for the heat of the day is over. Soon the night hawks will harpoon the sky. The desert is a solitary place, still, serene, endless.

The step-by-step progression shown in the illustrations (Figures 13-16) begins with a drawing—a simple arrangement of spaces and shapes—that allows us ample opportunity to experiment freely with washes and brush strokes. This might be a

FIGURE 13. DRAWING.

FIGURE 14. SKY.

good place to say that the illustrations in this book are included for the sole purpose of helping the reader develop his own technical facility. These are the tools, the scales, which will be used in individual creative expression.

Sky

Our first step is the sky (Figure 14). We are apt to feel that the arc of blue lies only above our heads, or begins out somewhere beyond the mountains. In reality the sky is all around us, touching and penetrating the earth at all points. We are very much part of it, and it is part of us. As we become aware of the nature of the sky in relation to the earth and ourselves, we will sense its character and our interpretation of it will be more significant.

The sky appears nearly white near the tops of the distant mountains, for we are looking northwest and the sun is on our left. The sky grades smoothly upward, darkening slightly as it lifts. It is also a little darker away from the light.

In Chapter 1 we experimented with a wash running from light to dark on dry paper; now we will try one on wet paper. Water is ladled on with a brush and evenly distributed from the base of the mountains over the entire sky area. A 2-inch flat brush does this most efficiently. If you wish, you may turn the board upside down and follow the same procedure as you did with a wash on dry paper, though it is not ordinarily necessary with this wash. As the water is distributed, hold the brush in a vertical position, the edge just touching the paper. An easy, full arm and body motion should be used, the weight of the body shifting slightly from the left foot to the right as the brush moves back and forth across the paper. You should be aware of an easy coordination between hand and wrist, arm and body.

Before going further, close your eyes and relax. Visualize the sky you are going to paint. When you have become really relaxed, fill the brush deeply with pigment and apply it in the center of the sky area. Lighten the wash with more water toward the base of the mountains and darken it at the top with more pigment as needed. Keep relaxed! A mistake is not too serious as the entire wash can be removed if necessary. To remove the wash, tip the board away from you at an acute angle and apply plenty of clean water at the base of the mountains, allowing it to flow across the paper until the pigment is all washed off. If, however, your wash seems right, tip the board and allow the pigment to grade itself; tilt slightly to the right to darken away from the light. Level the board and dry the edges and clips. Add a little sky pigment to the foreground to indicate that the sky is not something behind the mountains but that the earth and sky are one.

The graded wash is easier to handle on wet paper than on dry paper. There is no need to hurry. It will take a long time for the paper to dry. Easy does it. Move rhythmically and feel a part of the gradation you are painting.

Clouds

The paper—that is, the picture made thus far—must be perfectly dry before we begin our experiment with clouds, so while it is drying, let us consider the nature of diffused clouds (Figure 15). They are one of nature's greatest rhythms, the rhythm of water. Thus, they move, and being of the air, and air-borne, they float. Our aim is to symbolize their two characteristics, lightness and movement. Misty clouds have no hard edges and are generally larger, darker and more diffused overhead, lighter and more distinctly shaped in the distance.

When the paper is dry, wet it evenly again, holding the brush lightly and using only the edge. If you do not press down, very little of the pigment of the preceding work that has dried will be dislodged. Dry the paper slightly with the brush near the tops of the mountains so that here the diffusion will not be as great. Fill the brush with plenty of pigment, remembering that it will dry lighter, and that this will be especially true when it is diluted with the water already on the paper. Put in the large cloud in the upper right first, using the full width of the brush with a relaxed, free arm and body movement. The brush may be turned and pressed down slightly to give variations. This calls for a wrist movement combined with a tightening of the fingers. Next, move to the medium-size cloud, and then to the smaller one. Painting clouds is not quite as hazardous as it sounds; if all does not go well, they can be washed off while the paper is still uniformly wet and tried again, or even a third or fourth time. If the clouds are still not as you want them, wash the paper clean, let it dry flat and begin again with the sky. As you did before, relax. This time visualize the pattern of the clouds before you begin to paint. They may not come out just as you think they should, but it is a start in the right direction.

This loosely handled flowing approach to clouds is a thoroughly adaptable watercolor procedure and if the water is allowed to help, it will do better than half the work. But if you insist that the clouds be just your way, you will have plenty of trouble. When the cloud shapes are in, tip the paper to the right to create a movement, or toward you to let the clouds drip rain. Now watercolor will really help you more than you can help yourself.

Mountains

Our mountain has a serene, dignified shape so we will simplify its edge, maintaining its horizontal base to amplify its character and add composure to our picture (Figure 16). The distant mountains are lighter in value and appear to have more rounded contours. For this, we will experiment with washes that run from dark to light. Our previous washes have been graded from light to dark. When the sky area is dry, moisten the distant mountain shape from base to top. Fill the brush with pigment and paint the top edge of the mountain a value slightly darker than the sky. Round the contours. Clean the brush, pick up fresh water and with the brush semi-dry, pull pigment and water together, thus creating a graded wash that is slightly darker at the top and lighter at the base. Move to the next distant mountains, to the right, and repeat the procedure with more pigment this time, and slightly sharper edges. When the two areas are dry, we are ready to do the large mountain. Wet the area from the base of the mountain nearly to the top. This edge is important and you may want to change it as you go. The procedure from here on is the same; paint the top edge a dark value and as a line of repose, for this is the character of the mountain. This must be felt. When it is satisfactory, clean and dry the brush. Pull pigment and water together to indicate the soft mist rising from the desert floor. Lighten the mountain to the left and darken it to the right by lifting or adding pigment. If you wish to include a twister or dust devil, this may be done with a dry brush when the shine goes off the paper. (A twister or dust devil is a small cyclone generally spiraling along dry desert washes on hot days.)

FIGURE 15. CLOUDS.

FIGURE 16. MOUNTAINS

33

FIGURE 17. DISTANT TREES.

FIGURE 18. FOREGROUND.

Distant Trees and Bushes

Groups of trees and bushes in the distance lose their individual characteristics as they blend together and harmonize with each other (Figure 17). It is this mass that must be painted rather than the individual trees. The most significant feature of a mass of trees is its upper edge; the lower edge blends into the ground. The larger trees in leaf present crisp profiles, while others are more amorphous and blend into the mountain. To reduce this mass to its essential and thereby create an interesting watercolor symbol is our next experiment.

When the mountain area is dry, moisten the paper in spots slightly above the base line of the mountain. These areas should be fairly large but not flowing wet. The pigment will fuse into these spots creating soft edges. If too much water is used, the pigment will pull to the water edge and dry in a hard line, and the effect will be lost. If too little water is used, the pigment will not have a chance to be drawn out.

The brush is filled for a push stroke. It is held horizontally and manipulated as indicated in Figure 12 in the previous chapter. The flat edge parallels the base line of the mountains. As it is pushed upward, the pigment will fuse in the wet areas and be dry brushed in others, thus creating the characteristic edge in a direct watercolor manner.

The Desert Floor

Our next step is the desert floor and that spot of sunlight flecking a sandy area (Figure 18). It is usually easier to comprehend the character of the sky or mountains than of the earth. If we could feel Mother Earth as terra firma, solid and substantial, an enduring foundation upon which we walk and which supports buildings and vegetation, it would be easier for us to symbolize. The desert floor was once the bottom of a great ocean and though it has become leveled and eroded, it still maintains its flat, firm character.

Apply water to the foreground about one-fourth of an inch from the base line of the mountain. We will attempt to rough-brush the dry area, thus indicating the sunlit, sandy spot; then execute a flat but varied graded wash, that gets darker as it comes forward, to indicate the desert floor. The brush is loaded for a rough brush stroke. Held under the hand, the brush moves horizontally from left to right, as shown in Figure 8, one-fourth of its width in the dry area, three-fourths in the wet. If all goes well, elevate the brush to the vertical position, join the pigment to the rough brushing and move the wash forward. If the stroke is not successful, quickly turn the dry brushing into part of the graded wash, and when the paper is dry, try again. As you are painting, think of the desert floor creatively. See it and feel it as it was originally—a flat, barren ocean bed—for this is its dominant characteristic.

The roll of the foreground, the bushes and grasses come next. Here we will have our greatest trouble; suddenly we may want to deviate from our interpretive road and become illustrators, or begin painting in a manner well suited to a naturalist's manual. It is fun to paint every leaf and every twig but this is not for us, so let's not get bogged down here. It is better to say a few things that are significant than a number of things that have no meaning. Divide the foreground horizontally into three shapes—large, medium and small. The large shape might be the central open area; the medium, the roll of ground to the left; the small, the bank in the near right

foreground. As you divide, remember you are looking down on this area. We will not discuss perspective in detail, but a few suggestions may be helpful at this point. Note that your horizon line is near the base of the mountain. Two perspective points should be used. If these are located, it will be easier to indicate lines for brush strokes to follow.

We begin with the roll of earth to the left. Water is rough brushed on in the direction that the strokes are to follow. The roll of the ground should be felt as the water is applied. Visualize yourself walking over it, stepping up from the flat area to the rise and walking on level ground again. Pigment is applied and the nearest section slightly darkened. Some of the rough brush direction may be lost but this can be put in later, after the area is dry. At the far edge of the roll, indicate some distant bushes with push strokes. Let them blend into the ground but keep the top edge characteristic. Do the shaded side of the bank, letting the top edge round in a soft transition, and keeping the bottom edge distinct. Wait for a drying period. Moisten a few spots along the bank where you want more bushes. Use push and flip strokes and

FIGURE 19. FINISHED PAINTING.

edge lines. Remember that one edge should be distinct, the other diffused. It is basically a play of one characteristic shape against another just as the mountain was played against the sky, and the trees against the mountain. Use a corner of the brush for the yucca to indicate the fronds as they follow the growth of the plant from the center out.

Many watercolors are ruined in the last five minutes, so if it is late and you are tired, this is a good place to stop for the day. Mat your watercolor and put it up where you can see it and study it. Then leave it. When you come back to it, you will see it with a new enthusiasm.

And finally we come to the darks in the foreground. These are most important for it is here that paintings are usually balanced. Try putting them in with charcoal first to be sure they are where you want them. Use a little restraint and do not make the mistake of overworking your painting. When the last darks are finally in, you will be surprised and pleased to see how the mountain and sky recede and your painting suddenly comes to life (Figure 19).

Questions and Answers.

Q. Is drawing unimportant? You say little about it.

A. Drawing certainly is important, This is a book on painting, however, and it seems best to stay pretty much with one subject. It is assumed that anyone who is painting has some knowledge of drawing.

Q. I have noticed that the sky darkens toward the zenith but have never observed it getting darker away from the sun. Is this always true?

A. It is difficult to say always, but when the sky is clear, this is true. Then, the sky appears lighter close to the sun and darker away from it.

Q. Can skies or clouds be painted with a 2-inch brush?

A. Yes. On full sheets a 3-inch brush is often used.

Q. Is there any rule about wetting the paper before painting?

A. This is a matter of analyzing the painting surface from the standpoint of what is to be said. In doing a graded wash, large areas and those requiring manipulation are generally moistened, smaller ones are painted on dry paper.

Q. My paintings look fine close up, but at a distance, they do not hold together. Why?

A. Stand back from your painting and reach out as you work instead of bending over. Step back and look at your painting often with your eyes almost closed. Move around during drying periods. Stand the painting up across the room and look at it before beginning again. Look at the painting in a mirror frequently. Use a reducing glass or a pair of opera glasses.

Q. Is it a good idea to visualize all areas before starting to paint?

A. Yes.

Q. Why do the edges of mountains appear more rounded in the distance?

A. Atmosphere has a tendency to pool light. It rounds and softens edges, making objects appear lighter in value and bluer in the distance. When a bush casts a shadow on a cement walk, the shape is leaf-like and angular near the bush; but as the shadow falls away, the shape becomes circular or sun-shaped. Seen in perspective, it becomes oval. It is the same principle.

Q. My paper buckles when a wash is put on. Water settles in the hollows and balloons form. Is there any way that this can be avoided or controlled?

A. This can be avoided by using heavier, handmade papers which have been stretched. Lightweight papers buckle more than heavier ones. Light, machine-made papers are the worst offenders. Stretching the paper helps. If water settles in hollows, it can sometimes be picked up by drying the brush thoroughly and touching the puddle with the corner of the brush. The hairs pull the water up by capillary attraction. This is an emergency measure.

Q. Do you set out fresh pigment at the beginning of a painting as oil painters do?

A. Yes. Pigment is at its best when it is fresh from the tube.

Q. What kind of paper do you ordinarily use?

A. Usually a 300-pound handmade paper which has a medium rough surface and is free from blemishes. If the paper is not sufficiently hard, it is glue-sized. Rabbit-skin glue is allowed to dissolve in water overnight and is then brought to a simmer in a double boiler. Three ounces of glue, or less, is used to a gallon of water. The papers are immersed in a tray and allowed to stand a couple of hours, then laid out on flat surfaces to dry. This is a nuisance but if one likes to work on a hard paper, and treats about a dozen sheets at a time, it isn't too bad. Be careful to use no more than three ounces of glue to a gallon of water or glue rings are apt to appear. Too little glue is better than too much.

Chapter 3

AS THE PAINTER SEES

There are many ways of seeing: you can use a telescope, microscope, magnifying glass, or prism, to mention a few. It is impossible to be bored if you have a magnifying glass and a prism close at hand. Look at the head of a dandelion amplified ten times and you will be swept into a world of exquisite beauty. Look through a prism at wet earth and you will see it glisten as though it were gold studded with jewels. The early Chinese so venerated prisms that only Mandarins were allowed to own them. But more stimulating and exciting than any of these ways of seeing is the art of seeing with awareness. As we develop this way, we will be refreshed and stimulated by the beauty of life around us.

As artists we not only see objects individually but we see them in mass; we are aware of a group of objects rather than an individual object. We see value in relation to mass, the big contrasts of light and dark, and the large color areas. We find ways of eliminating detail for the sake of the big over-all patterns, for composition, interpretation and expression are dependent on this kind of seeing. There are many ways to do this; probably the most common and simplest way is to squint—either with one or both eyes. Some painters use a blue or black glass to reduce values to their essential mass character. A Claude Lorrain glass is excellent for this purpose. Try holding your half-closed hand to your eye and look through the hole with one eye squinted and the other completely closed. Other painters look through finders or through a hole punched in paper. Still others look with one squinted eye through an opening formed by spreading and crossing the index and middle fingers of both hands. The purpose underlying all methods is the same—to reduce objects, value and color to their essentials, thus eliminating detail. Most painters squint at their work or devise some other way of maintaining the characteristic simplicity of the mass pattern.

Reducing glass effect

Mirror effect

Squinting effect

FIGURE 20. MAGNIFYING GLASS, PRISM. AND CLAUDE LORRAIN GLASS.

Another way an artist uses his eyes is to restrict his wide range of vision. Spread your arms far apart and look straight ahead. Wiggle your fingers and you will see that the eyes' range of vision is nearly 180 degrees. While this is fortunate if you are driving, it is difficult if you are painting. Although the average person can see within an angle of nearly 180 degrees without turning his head, he can only really comprehend what is seen in an angle of about 30 degrees. Subject matter should be selected that can be encompassed within this 30 degree angle. When this principle is violated the result is generally two or three compositions in one, with a complete lack of unity throughout. Do what you wish with your subject for interpretive or expressive reasons, but do stay within your 30-degree angle of vision.

If you close one eye and hold the cover of a penny match box (Diamond preferred) horizontally to your other eyelid, snug against the side of your nose or glasses, your vision through the opening will be limited to 35 degrees (Figure 21). Allow your little finger to cut off about one fourth of an inch from the far end, and 30 degrees will be obtained. If you are seeing more horizontally than you wish to

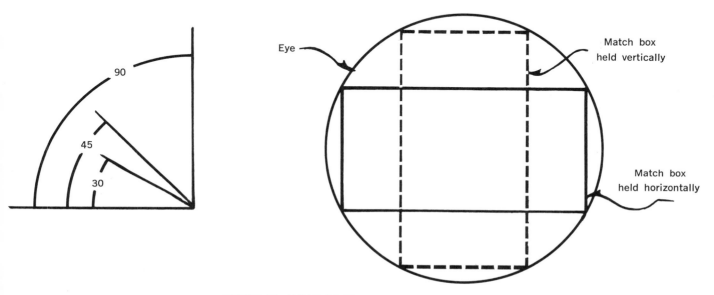

FIGURE 21. ANGLE OF VISION, MATCH BOX.

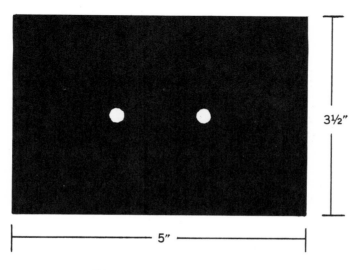

FIGURE 22. VALUE CARD.

FIGURE 23. MATCH BOX, VALUE CARD, AND GRAY SCALE.

include in the painting, move forward. If not enough, move back. If it is not possible to orient yourself in a reasonably satisfactory way to the subject, look for another subject. Hold the match box vertically to indicate what might be included vertically. Subject matter is thus related to a square or the equivalent of a circle, which is the way the eye sees. This in turn is related to the paper. If you are working on a square shape, all that is seen through the match box horizontally and vertically can be included. If the paper is rectangular and used the horizontal way, you would shorten the vertical range of sight. If the paper is used vertically, elimination would occur from the sides. The match box cover is not a compositional finder, although it is a compositional aid. Its purpose is to limit seeing to a comprehensive 30 degree angle. You may reduce the angle to 20 or even 15 degrees if you wish, but it should never be expanded beyond 30 degrees.

Values

Values—the word itself stirs thoughts that lie beyond the world of painting. The Chinese symbolize creativity with shapes of light and dark within an oval. The dark symbolizes the feminine principle and the light the masculine. The dark, rich earth from which the seeds spring speaks of the feminine. The light sky, the source of rain, reflects the masculine. In this symbol a spot of light is indicated in the dark and a spot of dark in the light.

The artist defines value as the measure or degree of light or dark, or the amount of light or dark reflected or absorbed by an object. Value means much more to him however, than this definition implies. He knows that as he paints, it may be the degree of light and the kind of light that stir him emotionally. Objects painted in brilliant sun will reflect quite a different emotion than the quiet mystery reflected by the same objects painted on a gray day in fog or rain.

Value, hue and intensity are the three dimensions of color. Value, which we think of as the most important part of color, is the degree of lightness or darkness of a color. Hue refers to the quality that enables us to distinguish one color from another—red, green, orange, blue, and so forth. Intensity, chroma, brilliance, and saturation—all words meaning the same thing—refer to the degree of brightness or dullness of a hue. To adequately describe a color, all three distinctions must be used. The *Munsell Book of Color,* by Albert Henry Munsell, explains the limitless variety of color obtainable within the boundaries of these three dimensions and is worthwhile for one who wishes to pursue the study at greater length.

We have investigated ways of seeing value only in relation to mass. Now we will be more specific in our appraisal as we add significance to our study of watercolor, and take another step along the road to interpretation and expression.

A piece of charcoal shaded by the hand and held against the elements in the landscape will establish a black standard and reveal the subtle value changes in the dark pattern. If you don't have a piece of charcoal, a shaded pencil or a stick will do. Telegraph poles and window battens may also be used as dark standards.

Our eyes are designed for many purposes as well as value appraisal. When their propensity for roving and range of vision is limited, and the side light is cut off, value, hue and intensity are seen more distinctly. Press the backs of your thumbs close against the sides of your nose and allow your index fingers to follow the contour of your eye sockets. As your fingers are pressed together, your hands form two openings which appear as one. It is like looking through an old-fashioned stereopticon viewer. As you view objects in this manner, you will see that form and color take on sharper and brighter aspects, and the diffused changes in value in both light and dark areas are seen more distinctly.

The color wheel grades in value from light yellow to dark violet. On a perfectly graded wheel, yellow-orange will be the same value as yellow-green, and red-violet the same as blue-violet. When one is painting a still life, the relation of value that occurs on the wheel is often a helpful way of determining the value of objects. Of course, considerable variation can occur and this comparison with the color wheel is only a beginning for observation.

Values are measured, that is, estimated, marked on the paper, and painted in a constant light. Inside light is naturally less intense than outside sunlight. Nevertheless, a unity of light, or a one-time-of-day feeling should be maintained in painting. If one is doing a still life, either in the studio or out-of-doors, the difference in value between the light and the dark side of an object will be consistent. If one finds that there are three different values from the light side of the lightest object to its shaded side, the same value relationship will be seen on all the other objects. This rule will seldom fail, but if it does, due to reflected light or mirror-like reflections on shaded sides, it is usually better to maintain a consistency than to interpret the slight difference in shaded areas that lessen the significance of light.

There is a rule saying, "All things being equal, the cast shadow on an object is darker than the shaded side." All things being equal means that the objects are identical in value, hue and texture. The cast shadow on a brick wall will probably be darker than the shaded side of the same wall. If, however, the cast shadow falls on a section of the wall that has been plastered, this will not be true. This is a fairly reliable rule and helps to create a consistency of light when it is followed.

An accurate way to judge value is with a value card (Figures 22 and 23). This simple device consists of a piece of black cardboard with two holes cut in it, as illustrated. The card makes it possible to eliminate objects or areas in a landscape that cause difficulty in value appraisal. For example, if you wished to make a careful comparison between the value of the low sky and the foreground, the intervening mountains, trees, and houses would bias your judgment. The value card may be held close to the eye or at a distance as desired. With one eye closed, place one opening in the value card on the low sky, and the other on the foreground. The two areas can now be more easily compared since everything between the low sky and the foreground has been eliminated by the space between the two holes.

There is one value rule so unchanging that it is referred to as "the three laws of light." Seldom, if ever, does one see this relationship broken. When a white box is held against the sky, the side in direct sunlight will be lighter than the blue sky, and the shaded side will be darker. When the box is held against the light, both sides will be darker than the sky. When the box is held with two sides in light, they both will be lighter than the sky. If one is working with architectural subjects in sunlight, the value relation between the sunlit side of a light building, the sky and shaded side of the building is a vital one for him to establish. Once this is done, it is the key to other value relations. This rule applies to sky, not clouds.

The nature of watercolor is such that its characteristic beauty is best reflected in light and dark value areas. Middle value is the land of uncertainty and seldom reflects watercolor at its best. It is important to have the value scale well fixed in our minds so that we can record the variety of values in the light and dark range that we see in nature, and also so that we may avoid the middle range in painting. Needless to say middle value does exist in nature, but in watercolor it is usually either lifted to a high range, lowered to a darker range, or eliminated completely. Our next step therefore is to make a value scale.

The average eye sees about 11 distinct variations in value, including black and white. Our scale is arranged accordingly. The dimensions for laying it out are given in Figure 24. The painting procedure is as follows. First, paint the black strip as dark as you can get it. Next, wet the Number 1 area and apply a small amount of pigment near center, adjusting by adding water or pigment, or lifting with a dry

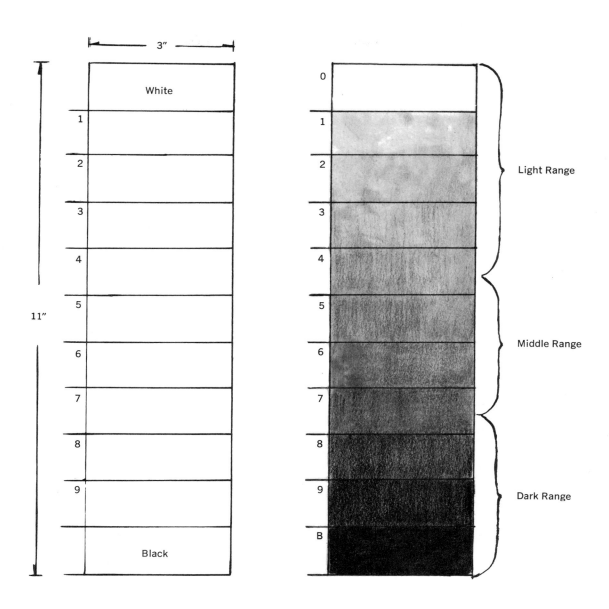

FIGURE 24. VALUE SCALE.

brush. Work from the center to the edges. Do not sample on another sheet but work directly on the paper. When you think the Number 1 value is correct, dry the area. See the change in value as it dries and if you think it is too light, paint it again. Before going to the Number 2 value, the first area should be dry. Don't skip around; wait for drying periods. Now proceed with value Number 2 as with value Number 1, using a little more pigment this time. Note how deceptively dark the pigment appears when it is wet. Dry the area and go on to value Number 3. The steps from 4 to 9 are identical in procedure with 1, 2, and 3. You will see that the change, due to drying, is not as great in the lower half of the scale.

A more useable value or gray scale can be made by flowing an evenly graded light to dark wash over a fairly heavy piece of 12-by-15-inch paper. Cut the sheet in half and divide the two pieces into strips about 2 inches wide. Select from this assortment an evenly graded group and staple the set together, as shown in Figure 23.

Questions and Answers.

Q. Where can one buy a magnifying glass and prism?

A. A 10X Hastings Triplet, which is a good magnifying glass, made by Bausch and Lomb Optical Company, Rochester, N. Y., can usually be purchased from a store handling engineering and drafting supplies. Or write Bausch and Lomb. My prism was purchased from a jeweler.

Q. May camera finders be used to establish the 30-degree angle of vision?

A. A camera finder usually has a much wider range than 30 degrees, though you might be able to find one.

Q. I have seen painters turn their backs to their subject, bend over and look through their legs. Is this another way?

A. Yes, and surprisingly enough a very good one if you are not sensitive to by-standers' remarks.

Q. Why must all three dimensions, value, hue and intensity, be used to adequately describe a color?

A. To describe the color of an apple, one might say, "It is a light, bright red." Light refers to value, bright to intensity, red to hue. There may be further amplifications of the color description but the adjectives used can only apply to value, hue or intensity.

Q. What if one said, "The apple is a vermilion color"?

A. Fine. Now it will be necessary to describe vermilion. It is only when it is known what is meant by vermilion in relation to value, hue and intensity that the color description is acceptable.

Q. Are there not some watercolorists who paint in middle value?

A. Yes, and very successfully. But it takes a great deal of know-how and experience. In addition, many watercolors you might think are painted in middle value are actually middle or low intensity, and either dominantly light or dominantly dark.

Q. When painting, why not test the values first on another piece of paper?

A. In painting, value, hue and intensity exist only in relation to adjacent painted areas. Adjustment should therefore occur on the paper so that a proper relation can be achieved. For this reason the practice of mixing right on the paper is encouraged and the practice of testing on another piece of paper discouraged. Testing is really a guessing procedure which is an impractical watercolor approach. Starting with a scale and mixing on the paper eliminates guessing and establishes the basis of a controllable watercolor method. The only testing that is advisable is a rough brush stroke. This stroke cannot be altered easily, and until one is proficient with a brush, it might be permissible.

Q. What is meant by saying that value, hue and intensity exist only in relation to adjacent areas?

A. Paint three identical squares of light vermilion. Surround one with a painted frame of dark green, another with a frame of yellow and the third, one of dark vermilion. Note how the appearance of the identical vermilion squares changes and you will see why value, hue and intensity exist only in relation to adjacent areas.

Chapter 4

FIELD EQUIPMENT

Sooner or later, the call of the outdoors will lure the landscape artist. His studio is the place to experiment, to study, and the place for executing paintings that are too technically difficult to do in the field. But the field is where he gathers inspiration. Under the sky expression emerges freely and watercolors are fresh and spontaneous; here the painter is more actively aware. What is so generously given by nature and reflected by the watercolorist in his outdoor painting can seldom be recaptured inside, and few artists attempt it. The character of watercolor itself is compatible with the sky, the air, the sun and rain. Of course, there are hazards—the wind, cold, rain, dust, mosquitoes and burning sun. Still, it is worth facing them all, for we are of nature and painting in the field establishes a bond of unity and harmony with the whole of creation as nothing else does.

The kind of equipment used in the field is a personal matter but the choice is important; it will have much to do with one's enjoyment and success when painting out-of-doors. Ordinarily selections of equipment are made on the basis of comfort and efficiency. However, comfort for one person is not necessarily comfort for the next, and efficiency must be related to the locale in which one is painting, as well as to the materials he is using. The following suggestions are based on tried and proven experiments. Some are specifically directed to painting in the Southwest; many can be used any place.

A first step toward establishing comfort and efficiency for outside painting is to consider what constitutes these two factors for you inside. Look over all the things you use and reduce them to a minimum. Consider the brushes you need most often in relation to the size of the paper you will be working on. Think of how much Kleenex you use in a day's painting. Cut that big art gum eraser in half, and then in half again. Fill the pockets of your watercolor box, selecting the few pigments that must be squeezed out fresh when used, and putting the others aside. Unfortunately, there are a few things that must be left behind—the hair drier, the shade, that fine north light and probably the big pail. You will have to make reasonable substitutions for these indoor assets.

FIGURE 25. THE WATERCOLOR BAG HOLDS EVERYTHING.

The next step is to find something to hold all your treasures that will be easy to carry. A watercolor bag serves this purpose adequately. The one illustrated is made of 12-ounce canvas and is 23 inches long, 18 inches high and 4½ inches wide (Figure 25). The straps go over the left shoulder, leaving the left hand free to support the bottom of the bag when necessary. It holds a portfolio for watercolor and drawing paper, a stool, a sketch pad and the board for stretched paper. Inside pockets are designed to hold two water containers (pint Skippy peanut butter jars will do) clips, a small pack of Kleenex, paint rag and watercolor box. Other necessities, such as brushes, eraser, pencils, charcoal, thumb tacks, and extra tubes of paint are in the bottom of the paint box. It is a good idea to service the watercolor bag after every painting trip so that you will have everything ready for the next time. Be sure to have your name on all your equipment and include your address on the bag. A large knapsack is sometimes preferred to a watercolor bag, especially if there is hiking or climbing to be done. Remember that you can do only a limited number of watercolors in a day and it is foolish to carry more truck than you need. However, a tool kit kept in the car filled with an assortment of things you think you might need, such as a water jug and a few sheets of paper, will give you a feeling of security.

TWO WINDMILLS
Courtesy Mr. and Mrs. Ross Stefan

FIGURE 26. SETUP FOR A SUNNY DAY.

FIGURE 27. STOOL AND KNEELING PAD.

When working outside on a stool, the watercolor bag is placed on the ground, with portfolio and paper on top to keep them clean. The setup of material is identical with the inside order established, and for the same reasons.

If one prefers to sit rather than stand when painting, a light, comfortable and strong painting stool is just the thing. The one illustrated is made of 1-inch aluminum tubing and heavy canvas and is 12 inches high—which is just about right for the average person (Figures 26, 27). When the stool is placed about 15 inches from the edge of the watercolor bag, and one sits erect, the left elbow resting on the left knee, the edge of the brush held in the vertical position should just touch the paper. The elbow will be slightly and naturally bent, the arm relaxed. When painting on a stool, keep the back straight and bend from the hips. The elbow should be kept on the knee to assure this position. Hold the neck firm but relaxed; bend forward as though you were balancing an apple on your head.

A good substantial stool is the Scotsman Seat Shell Box (made by the American Gas Machine Company, Albert Lea, Minnesota). It has a foam rubber seat which can be raised to three levels ranging from 10 to 14 inches. The seat turns which is an advantage, for body movement in painting is facilitated. The inside of the box makes good storage space. The only difficulty is that the stool is heavy so if you plan to use it, you will want to stay near your car.

54

FIGURE 28. UMBRELLA AND SHADE DEVICES.

Many painters prefer to stand as they work. This calls for more equipment but it is worth it if one is more comfortable. A useful easel, light and easily adjusted to uneven ground may be constructed by modifying a photographer's tripod. These have the advantage of swivels that tip, turn and lock, and can be easily broken down for limited studio space. The main disadvantage is that they must be used with boards, one for half sheets, another for full sheets. There are many kinds of easels ranging from fairly heavy wooden ones to others made of lighter aluminum. When using an easel, a light stool and a piece of Upsom board will do to hold the water containers and paint box. Card tables are good, especially the light, inexpensive wooden type. A rock placed on the table top will keep it from taking off.

In the Southwest, and especially in Arizona, creating shade for the paper is a real problem, for here the sun rules the sky nearly every day, and there are no spreading chestnut trees springing from the desert. To paint with one's paper in the sun here, or anywhere for that matter, produces nothing but a bad watercolor and a headache. Paints should also be shaded as the sun can harden pigment quickly. There is nothing better for this than a large umbrella, preferably gray, that swivels or tips at the top and is light and strong. Unfortunately they are hard to find. The one illustrated is an old one made in England that has been recovered in light gray sail cloth (Figure 26). The sun through it does not change the color of the paper. The

FIGURE 29. CARD TABLE AND SHADE APPLIANCE.

metal stake made from light-weight angle iron has a sharpened end which pushes into the ground easily, even when the terrain is rocky. The post is secured to the stake by thumb screws.

A simple devise for securing shade is a piece of coat hanger wire curled at the ends to hold the portfolio open (Figure 25). This device can be used effectively especially when working into the light in late afternoon. A larger more efficient device for producing shade can be made with four canvas stretchers, some gray cloth or window shade material and a number of other odds and ends, as shown in Figure 28. This piece of equipment is light, effective and practical. It can also be attached to a card table (Figure 29).

Two ice bags make fine water containers for they are light, do not break or upset and will rest securely on any spot of ground (Figure 30). The water is always near the top of the containers which will fit nicely into the watercolor bag when the day's painting is over. The small ones which hold about a pint of water are large enough. If one is careful always to wash the brush in one container and pick up clean water from the other, he can paint all day with this supply. If they are blown up after each use, and allowed to dry upside down, they will last longer. Tie them together with a leather thong or light rope and they will be easier to carry and not as easy to lose.

It is often more difficult to dry paper outside than indoors where a dryer is available. If you are near your car, you can use the heater or start the motor and hold your painting upside down over the engine. This really does the job fast. A fan is a light and useful accessory. The woven straw ones used by the Mexicans to brighten their cooking fires are efficient, nice to handle, and good to look at.

FIGURE 30. WATER CONTAINERS.

Photograph by
Jay Sternberg

Questions and Answers.

Q. Is working from sketches as satisfactory as painting directly from nature?

A. Nearly, but not quite. You may gum up the outside painting, but you will still have a quality that can be obtained in no other way. No landscape painted inside can compare in freshness and spontaneity with one that is painted on location.

Q. Is salt water ever used in painting?

A. Yes, but it is not recommended. Pigments discolor and darken, and it is hard on brushes.

Q. How do you put your name on a paint brush?

A. Scratch your name on the ferrule of the large ones and notch the others.

Q. Should one work from photographs?

A. No. It would be better to make the roughest kind of a pencil note or devote the time that might be required to take a photograph, to looking. Expression and interpretation are based on what one feels as much as what he sees. Photographs are apt to lead to copying and therefore do the expressive painter more harm than good.

Q. It is difficult for me to either sit on a stool or stand when I paint. Could I use a light chair and raise the paper to a higher level?

A. Yes. A chair without arms is best. Remember that free arm movement and body coordination are necessary.

Q. How can the watercolor bag, portfolio and paper be raised a little higher?

A. Put a rolled up jacket under the bag, or use a low table, similar to the ones used for reading or writing in bed. A small light stand could be made to put your portfolio on. There are innumerable ways.

Q. Can one kneel on the ground in oriental fashion when painting?

A. Yes. There is probably no better way other than standing, for all the principles inherent in free arm movement and body coordination are easy to apply. Kneeling has it all over standing as far as equipment goes.

Q. I am not clear about the portfolio. Will you explain it more in detail?

A. The portfolio is made of two pieces of 3/16-inch Upsom board and is 15 x 22 inches. It is fastened together the horizontal way with heavy masking tape. About a quarter of an inch should be left between the boards when they are taped so that they will fold. The outside surfaces are painted white. Paper can be clipped to this portfolio but it can not be stretched on it.

Chapter 5

VALUE

INTERPRETATION

Two hundred years before the American Revolution, men of Spain followed the valley of the Santa Cruz river northward. With armor clinking and crosses held on high, they passed a spot along the way where today nestles the little village of Tubac. In 1700 Father Kino came to build a chain of missions from Magdalena to Tucson, and to tell the world that the Bay of Southern California was not the Pacific ocean. In 1752 a Presidio was established, soldiers marched, men tilled the soil and grazed their cattle, mines were opened and Tubac grew to be a city. As the years rolled on, the Yankees came to join the Spaniards, Mexicans and Indians to build and to destroy. Trees were felled and the grass grew sparse. Game disappeared and the Santa Cruz began to sink into the earth. Above in the high ranges of the Santa Rita mountains, the Apaches watched and waited. One day their time came and for many years afterward the valley was still. The adobe houses melted back to the earth and tumbleweed had its way.

TUBAC AT NIGHT
Courtesy Edward and Eve Morgan

In territorial times Tubac rose again and a man, who must have had a glint of Sweden in his eye, built a church. Its clean facade and steep roof spoke of snow loads that were never to be.

Perhaps some time you will see the church at Tubac in the light of a Hallowe'en moon. As the arabesques embroidered on its walls whisper tunes of other days, you will hear the murmur of mass chanted under the cottonwoods, and the zesty songs of Conquistadores. Cowboy ballads, the music of the covered wagons and Forty-niners will drift through the night air. You will hear the soft insistent beat of Indian drums and dancing moccasined feet. Through it all will be the strum of a Mexican guitar, for the tradition of the Southwest comes from south of the border.

Today the church glistens in the sun. Its white front and stocky tower saber the blue sky. Inside it is still and cool, and one thinks of quiet New England churches. But here also is the color and tinsel of Mexico, relieving and disturbing the tranquility at the same time. Here the Mexicans, Indians and Yankees lace hands in prayer and in tradition.

It is ten o'clock in the morning. The sky is blue, the air is clear. The sun strikes the white church with dazzling brilliance. It is the same sun that Father Kino felt as he worked, the same blue sky that arched above him. Despite the changing years, the same joy of life is reflected, the same sparkle, the same resilience. Before we pick up our brushes and try to express what we feel about the warmth and brilliance of the day, let us pause to discuss some basic elements of composition.

Composition

Whenever we touch the fabric of art in any one place, we touch the whole garment. It is impossible to consider any one aspect of painting, such as value, irrespective of the whole. As soon as we begin a painting, composition enters in, for this is a factor common to all forms of artistic expression. Since this book is about watercolor, it is not possible for us to delve deeply into the principles of composition, but we will touch on the matter lightly as it concerns watercolor and suggest that the student reads books on composition that cover the subject more specifically. Although there are many theories of composition, in essence they all deal with three elements—balance, movement, and space. Their goal is creating unity and harmony through the juxtaposition of forms and colors.

Watercolor is an easy-flowing spontaneous medium and by its very nature does not lend itself to a completely analytical, systematized or regimented approach. When the medium is bound by too many compositional rules, it loses its characteristic freshness and spontaneity and becomes rigid and awkward. If compositional principles are totally ignored, however, one's watercolor will suffer from a lack of unity and harmony. While the watercolorist should paint in a free, easy and abandoned manner, behind this abandon must lie a firm understanding of composition.

Watercolor is like a game of chess; one move on the board calls for a balanced move. The watercolorist's thought must be for the whole paper as it develops compositionally and he should never start a painting with the idea of making the parts fit a predetermined pattern. In landscape, for example, one can easily see that a free-flowing sky is not absolutely controllable, and since this is so the other elements in the composition should not be rigidly fixed. They should be subject to modification in relation to what has happened in the sky. If one were painting in oil or any other opaque medium, he might work from scaled dummies to larger finished paintings. Murals are usually done this way, the dummy being expanded to exactly fit the wall. For the watercolorist such a procedure would be fairly impossible. Try copying one of your own watercolors exactly and you will see why forgery in this field is almost impossible.

Perhaps the greatest compositional asset to the watercolorist is a feeling for relationships of form and color. If principles of composition are applied analytically, the watercolor will always lack spontaneity and freshness. It is important therefore to develop a sensitivity for these relationships; it leads not only to successful compositions but to better watercolors generally.

When driving through the country, watch the mountain shapes as they impinge one on another. In doing this, you will become aware that at certain times the relationships are quite perfect and at other times they are not. Observe houses, trees, telegraph poles, roof tops and chimneys against the sky. You will see that some relationships of patterns and overlapping forms are pleasing and others are not. Slowly but surely you will develop an awareness of satisfying compositional relationships. These adventures in aware seeing are highly important for the water-colorist and eventually will become the key to successful, free composition and easy, fluid watercolors.

When a painting is laid out, essential compositional principles are often used to achieve a generally satisfying arrangement of parts in relation to the whole and to attain a basic structural unity. This is frequently done in an analytical manner. As soon as the first washes are applied, however, a strange but necessary mental change usually takes place in the painter. The thinking mind is somehow turned down and the aware nature takes over. This does not mean that the mind is empty. It simply means that the aware nature gains ascendancy and draws those things from the mind that are necessary to achieve satisfactory compositional relationships. If you are aware of how you achieved a satisfactory compositional watercolor passage, you will see that this is about what happens. You will also see that your experiments with aware seeing are beginning to pay off.

It is interesting to note how often the unified significance of life is expressed in terms of three, from such utilitarian objects as a knife, fork and spoon to concepts of the sun, moon and stars. Morning, noon and night symbolize the day; father, mother and child the family. Religious theologies are replete with this trilogy. From the largest concepts to the smallest, the eternal triangle is always with us. In the world of art, this same relationship of three occurs again and again. Value, hue and intensity constitute the dimensions of color and all color is derived from the three primaries, red, yellow and blue. The consideration of landscape painting evolves about three planes, the sky, distance and foreground. Another interesting factor related to the recurring sequence of three is that usually any given triumvirate will be oriented in degrees of first, second and third importance or large, medium and small. This is easily seen with a knife, fork and spoon. Consider red, yellow and blue. It is true, all seem of equal importance in relation to color, but if we made a painting in which all three hues were given equal space and strength, we would probably have a watercolor that was neither unified nor harmonious. We can see how this works in our painting of the church at Tubac. If we painted our three planes, the sky, distance and foreground, all of equal interest, our watercolor would of course be unsatisfactory. If the church is to be the dominant element of interest, the sky and mountains must be subordinated.

Possibly the greatest advantage of this compositional approach for the water-colorist is that first, it is fast; second, and most important of all, it orients the painter's thinking to unified mass consideration. A painting is unified as the parts are significantly related in an orderly and harmonious way to the whole. This principle is not unique to the world of art. It is a universal principle. Pause a moment to consider the evolutionary pattern of our world. First, the swirling mass of nebulous gases; evolving from this emerged the waters and earth. Then the mountains and islands appeared and after untold centuries, plants, trees, fishes and

FIGURE 31. ON-THE-SPOT PHOTOGRAPH.

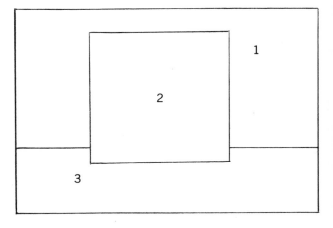

FIGURE 32. PAPER IS DIVIDED INTO THREE LARGE AREAS.

animals and finally human beings arrived. Always the creative pattern is from large to small. It is said that "mighty oaks from little acorns spring," but let's not forget that it is the creative pattern within the seed that forms the tree and not the seed itself.

If one wishes to follow the creative pattern when drawing for watercolor, it is well to remember that the large forms come first and the smaller ones follow. To begin with the little things first, hoping to achieve unity by the proper disposition of these small parts, one is only courting trouble.

The photograph of Tubac was taken at the approximate location from which the watercolor was painted (Figure 31). The rectangle drawn on the photo indicates what could be seen through the match box at this spot. Since the average camera has a focal spread of 60 degrees or more, photographs for painting reference should be taken at closer range than the actual painting location.

The front of the church, including the tower but not the side, is almost square. Compositionally, in relation to the emotion to be expressed, the first step is to relate this square to the paper in a pleasing, balanced manner. The principle of three was used with the thought in mind that the area of interest would be the church. When the square was made smaller, it seemed too diminutive. When it was drawn larger, it appeared cumbersome and overpowering. When it felt expressively right in relation to size and seemed well placed in relation to balance, it was drawn emphatically on the paper, together with a horizontal line to indicate the base of the mountains as indicated in Figure 32. The paper was thus divided into three spaces, the large sky area marked 1, the medium-sized church square numbered 2 and the small foreground area, 3. The first step seems fairly simple but actually more effort and

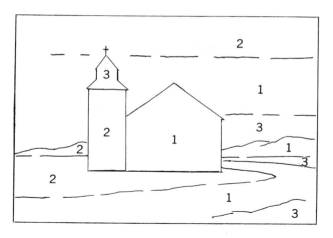

FIGURE 33. DIVISION OF CHURCH FRONT, SKY,
DISTANT PLANE, AND FOREGROUND.

FIGURE 34. PERSPECTIVE LINES INDICATE
DEPTH OF CHURCH.

thought was expended here than in any of the other developments. As goes the first shape space relationships in a watercolor, so goes the painting.

The next step was to delineate the flat front of the church and divide it into three spaces, a large, medium and small, indicated by the numbers, 1, 2 and 3 (Figure 33). The sky was then divided in a similar way as indicated, then the distant plane and the foreground. If the first step is satisfactory, the second will not be difficult.

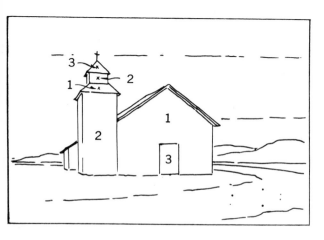

FIGURE 35. FACADE IS DIVIDED INTO THREE AREAS.

FIGURE 36. FIRM INDICATIONS ARE ADDED.

65

The third step was to indicate the depth of the church through perspective. The horizon line was located near the base of the church. One vanishing point was found to be close in to the left and the other far out to the right. Figure 34 indicates the approximate position of these points. When the depth of the church was indicated and the front corrected, the facade was divided into an interesting relation of large, medium and small areas by eliminating one window and modifying the shape of the bell-tower slightly (Figure 35).

The final step was done quite freely and easily (Figure 36). At this stage, it is more a matter of selection and elimination than anything else. Generally, when basic relationships in the large areas are well established, detail falls in place easily.

Value Appraisal

Our next step is to determine the values we see in nature. We note the position of the sun and the direction of its movement. The church faces slightly northeast, the sun is behind us and a little to the left. In about two hours the whole front will be in shadow. An arrow is marked on the paper to indicate the direction of light.

We have our value card at hand, and the match box cover which has given us our 30-degree angle of vision. Our next consideration is the large value relationships, the big differences between the light and dark pattern. These may be quite easily seen by looking through a dark glass or partly closed eyes. We see that the white church, sky, foreground and mountains, although differing considerably in value are all in the light value range. Compare the values with the value scale in Figure 24. In fact, nearly everything hit by sunlight is in a value range not lower than 3½. The shade and shadow areas are in the range from 7 to 9 with the exception of the shadow on the white facade of the church which is around middle value, and the sunlit sides of the tower roof, which have been painted black and are below middle value. It is better to interpret these middle values in a slightly higher range to amplify the sparkle of the day. We note that the white building is lighter than the blue sky and that the shadow is darker. If the value of the shadow is to be raised, the value relation must still be maintained.

We use our value card now to appraise the subtle changes in value occurring in both the light and dark patterns. As these values are determined, they are marked on the paper with pencil, beginning with the lightest and ending with the darkest (Figure 37). As the pencil marks will erase when the painting is finished, it is well to mark them boldly so that they can be easily seen, for the values will be painted in sequence beginning with the lightest.

If you are painting something in a gay, light, happy mood, sing as you work. Laugh. Know that your brush is dancing over the paper and that every stroke is an expression of what you feel. The sum total of those laughing, dancing strokes will add up to a painting that is happy and gay.

The first value painted was the front of the church marked 0 to 0+. Consult the key in Figure 37 for identification of value references that follow. Water was rough brushed on the surface and pigment introduced at the right hand side, away from the light. The wash was carried beyond the door and allowed to fuse with the water.

The next area was the road, marked 0 to 1. Water was distributed at the far end of the road and carried about half way down the surface. Pigment was applied in

FIGURE 37. VALUES MARKED.

FIGURE 38. VALUE 0 TO 3½ PAINTED.

FIGURE 39. VALUES 7 TO 9 PAINTED.

the water and lifted until the value was right, then carried forward into the water. Rough brushing, following the perspective lines in the road, occurred in the close foreground.

The sky was painted next with a graded wash running from light to dark on moistened paper, then the mountains, a light Number 2 value, followed by the church tower, the roof and the door. These were done freely, though care was taken to keep the edges sharp, for such a treatment is suitable for painting architectural subjects.

Then came the grasses, bushes and light side of the tree, done with push strokes and flat rough-brushing, in values around 3 and 3½. The light values were all put in rapidly with flecks of white paper allowed to show through painted areas and plenty of white paper left exposed. When the paper was dry, the values were checked against a gray scale.

At this stage (Figure 38), our painting looks bland and uninteresting, and it should, for if there is too much contrast, the dark pattern—which will be the eye-attracting feature—will lose significance.

The palette was then cleaned and all excess water wiped up with Kleenex. The next series of values, the dark areas, called for more pigment than water (Figure 39). The first value painted was the cast shadow under the eaves of building and tower, 3½ at the edge, darker under the overhang. The cast shadow on the bell cupola of the tower was painted in value Number 7, then the shaded side of the grasses and tumble-weed in the same value. The shaded sides of the trees and fence posts were indicated in values ranging from 8 to 9.

Before putting in the last values and graphic delineations such as windows and doors, the over-all impact of the light and dark pattern was studied. After the dark values are painted in any watercolor, the light values often appear lighter than they should. Sometimes this happens because the high values have not been painted dark enough, at other times the keying of the darks against the lights makes them appear lighter. The front of the building and the road were rough-brushed for texture and to darken them a bit.

The last darks were put in and some textural suggestions on the tower roof and front of the building, and a telephone pole was added in the left distance to repeat the shape of the cross (Figure 40). These were done with a pointed brush.

An orderly procedure to follow generally for subjects such as this is painting all areas in sunlight first—which usually will take care of the values from 0 to 3½. Then paint the values in shade and shadow from 7 to 9. Third, check both the light and dark pattern for variety in value and undue contrast between the two. Fourth, add rough brushing, textural indications and small brush delineation.

Three Factors

Expressive painting is achieved through the balance of three factors. The first is know-how which is acquired by thinking, study and practice. The second factor is feeling. This has nothing to do with thinking or study but relates to our emotions. It is what we feel that we need to express. We often have the most wonderful and varied emotions that we would like to express in painting but without the ability or know-how, our results would be negligible. Feeling is a fundamental requisite to expression; without it there can be no expression.

FIGURE 40. FINAL DARKS AND GRAPHIC SUGGESTION.

There is also a third factor, an intangible. It reflects itself in a voice within us which says, "This is it," or again, "That isn't it." Whatever this factor is, it seems to know, and this knowing is not related to our mental understanding or to our emotions. We call this the knower. When these three factors—mind, feeling and knowing—are balanced and working smoothly, painting seems to go along easily and spontaneously, but when one is out of balance, painting becomes tedious and the results appear laborious. If expression is to be achieved, these three factors must be kept in operation. It is easy to forget that little inner voice and when we do, our difficulties multiply. It is well to remember that the inner voice must have something to relate its approval or disapproval to. Its yes and no, right and wrong, are related to what you feel at a specific time. For instance, if the subject you are about to paint makes you feel happy, if it seems full of light or has a sort of zing and zest about it, remember, it isn't the subject that feels that way. It is you. What you feel, you are; and what you are, you are trying to express. What you are trying to express is what your in-knower is talking about when it says, "That's it" or "That isn't it." These assertions are made with every stroke you put down in the continual now—now—now. The in-knower doesn't seem to be concerned with delayed fulfillment. It operates in a continual now. It follows that whatever feeling you are trying to express at the beginning of a painting should be held to, for if you start out in a gay mood and later change to a somber one, the in-knower will realize that unity and harmony are impossible to achieve, and will probably give up the project. This leaves you with only mental ability to work with and this is not enough to achieve your end—that of expression.

Questions and Answers.

Q. Why was the church reduced to a square? Why not begin with its characteristic shape?

A. When objects are reduced to basic or near basic shapes, one thinks in terms of pattern—which is desirable. Furthermore, objects are easier to construct when reduced to basic shapes.

Q. What is a basic shape?

A. Actually, there are only two, the circle and the square. Generally, however the rectangle and triangle are included, sometimes others. Basic shapes are thought of as flat. When they are distorted, cut off, halved or altered, they are called free shapes. When the illusion of a third dimension is given a basic shape, it is called a basic form. The circle becomes a sphere, the square a cube, the rectangle a cylinder, the triangle a pyramid, etc.

Q. Why was the arrow indicating the direction of light necessary?

A. It might be said that expression is achieved as light is interpreted, for it is often the quality and kind of light that stirs us emotionally. As light is forced, so is expression amplified. The arrow is a constant reminder of the direction of light. All areas, whether in the light range of value or the dark, are ordinarily lightened toward the source of light. Selection and transposition is based frequently on the direction of light. For instance, if dark textures are seen on the left hand wall of the church, they would be transposed to the right hand side. Forcing the direction of light also creates movement.

Q. What did we mean when we spoke of "interpreting the church?"
A. Our job as watercolorists is to interpret the shape of the church, its texture, and its value. If we can think of the church as an object that affords us the opportunity of interpreting light, the job will be more fun, and the painting will have greater expressive quality.

Q. Why the suggestion that we leave white flecks of paper showing in the light values but not in the darks?
A. Bright lights actually glint in areas hit by sunlight but when in shadow this is not possible.

Q. Would you suggest other ways by which a feeling for balanced relationships in composition might be developed?
A. Cut a piece of paper or cardboard about 4 by 5½ inches. Take a half dollar, quarter, dime and a nickel and see how many satisfactory balanced arrangements you can make, keeping the coins separate from one another as you do so. Now add a few pennies and group some of the coins together as you repeat the experiment. Following this, take rectangular objects such as an eraser, pocket knife, match clip and the stub of a pencil and continue. Now group rectangular and circular objects together and see what happens. If you find the project interesting, repeat it on a piece of gray paper and then on a black one. A lot can be learned about balanced relationships and composition in this manner.

A fun compositional experiment is to lay a stamp in the lower left-hand corner of an envelope and then address the envelope. Try the stamp in the lower right and upper left and then towards center and see how you are instinctively impelled to change the position of the writing to create a satisfactory balance.

It is interesting to study the doodling you do at the telephone in relation to spontaneous composition. Doing collages and mobiles is an excellent way to develop a feeling for compositional relationships and balance.

Q. I frequently lose the compositional feel of a painting, especially toward the end. Could you explain why this happens?
A. It is hard to say, but possibly you have become tired without realizing it. When this happens, one is inclined to rationalize his painting rather than feeling its compositional structure in an aware way. Also at the end of a painting, small brush work is generally called for and one is apt to bend over the paper too closely and too carefully apply the strokes. When this is done, the tendency is to lose contact with the painting as a whole. The little lines are then unrelated to other areas on the sheet and so the unity and compositional integrity of the watercolor is broken.

71

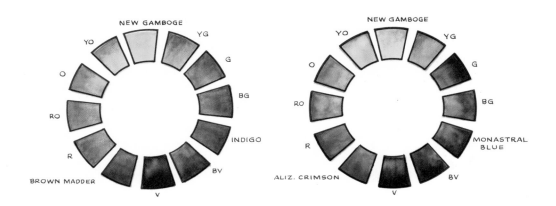

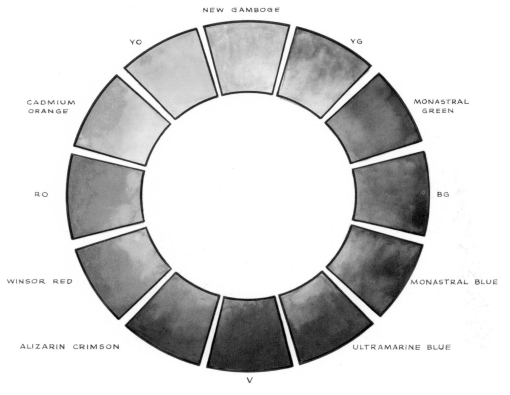

FIGURE 41. COLOR WHEELS.

Chapter 6

PIGMENTS AND PALETTES

Mystery and beauty surround pigments. We merge a bit of blue and green together on a wet palette and the two blend into a delicate turquoise as one hue drifts into the other. Fingers of blue and green reach out and as they meet, they change as if by magic. Our imaginations sweep us into another world as we tip our palettes and let the water flow. We dream of ocean currents swirling in tropical waters. Forms appear and disappear, sea-weed and rocks, a fish emerges and vanishes. We add more green and some alizarin and pull the two together with a brush. Opalescent grays appear as the colors fuse and we see the heart-shaped blossom of a banana plant grow and change. We wonder why the grays occur. The pearl-like gray shimmering and pulsating on the white surface of the palette tinged with red in some areas and green in others, but still something of its own and beautiful in itself. We realize that the gray will never return to red and green. Mysteriously, a new appearance has been created and we are filled with wonder. Pigments are beautiful in themselves; on a palette and on paper, they are magic in our hands, but magic that must be understood. Even though we are aware of the wonder of pigments, we must know their nature and how to use them; this is part and parcel of the world of painting.

There are two kinds of pigments, those that are transparent or staining and those that are opaque or precipitating. Since both kinds are included on our palettes, it is particularly important to know which kind we are using and how they differ. When light rays are reflected from a surface painted with a transparent pigment, the rays penetrate the film of color and reflect from the white paper back through the pigment with luminosity. When light is returned from an opaque color, it is reflected from the granule of the pigment only. As watercolor is dependent on white paper for its source of light, transparent pigments are best suited to the water-colorist's needs. The more white paper is allowed to reflect luminosity, the more resilient in color the painting will be. This is especially true in the high range of value.

Pigments have varying ranges of value. Black has the longest value range of any pigment, yellow the shortest. All other colors vary between these two. Pigments also have varying degrees of strength in mixtures. For example, the yellows are weak compared with the reds and blues; it takes much more yellow than blue when the two are mixed to make green. The better we understand these differences, the less difficulty we will have in combining colors. Pigments also vary in relation to black content. There is no black or white in the spectrum, and these two achromatic colors and all the hueless family of grays are known as neutrals. Since nature creates grays unendingly, we will want to use gray in painting. We will be better able to get a vibrant luminous quality of light if we know the content of black in the pigments we are using. The color wheels and the "Know Your Pigments" chart, while not exhaustive, will help us understand pigments more fully (Figures 41 and 42).

Let us experiment with our pigments, starting with a stack of paper half-sheet size, and a large palette. Squeeze out pigment as you need it. Make large color swatches, running each one from its lightest to its darkest value, using plenty of water in the light areas and plenty of pigment in the dark. In Figure 43 color swatches are reproduced in black and white. Note in your chart where the color is the brightest in relation to the amount of water used. Diluting a pigment lowers its brightness; using too much pigment ordinarily does the same thing. Between these two extremes is the spot of full intensity. This varies with each pigment. Note the opacity or transparency of the pigment and what it does when it dries. Check the value range with your gray scale. Observe that raw sienna and raw umber are yellow and that burnt sienna and burnt umber are orange. When the swatches dry, try washing them out with a brush and a sponge to determine their degree of staining power.

Brand names are given on the chart (Figure 42). These are my favorites, but one should choose the brands he prefers. All manufacturers make good pigments as well as pigments that are not as good. In this country, the United States Bureau of Standards requires that the content and nature of the pigment be printed on the tube. This is not required in all countries. If you will read the printing on your tubes and get the free literature distributed by manufacturers, you can avoid colors that are fugitive.

Watercolors are no more fugitive than oils, nor are they as subject to chemical change. Though no pigment is completely permanent, the color in many of the Chinese watercolors has altered only slightly in hundreds of years, even though the materials on which they were painted have discolored. The best way to select pigments for permanency is by light testing. This is done by painting strips of color over a sheet of paper, then covering half and allowing the sun to work on the exposed areas for 36 to 48 hours. In the Southwest, this is a brutal test.

We have determined the nature of our pigments in relation to transparency, value range, black content and staining power. Now let us see what they do in combination in relation to their varying strengths. If we desire luminosity in painting, the most desirable pigments are the transparent ones that have a long value range and no black content. Transparent pigments that have a short value range and no black content are also useable. Others that are transparent and have a long value range, but contain black, should be reserved for low-intensity color situations. They should be most cautiously used if bright light is to be interpreted. Our best selections then are new gamboge, Monastral green, Monastral blue, ultramarine, alizarin crimson, burnt sienna, indigo and brown madder.

FIGURE 42. KNOW YOUR PIGMENTS.

Pigment	Make	Opaque	Value Range	Black Content	Staining Power	Transparent
Winsor red	Winsor & Newton		Medium	Zero	High	Yes
Cadmium red & vermilion	Winsor & Newton	Yes	Short	Zero	Slight	
Cadmium orange	Grumbacher	Yes	Short	Zero	Slight	
New gamboge	Winsor & Newton		Short	Zero	Slight	Yes
Cadmium yellow	Pottinger	Yes	Short	Zero	Slight	
Mixed green			Long	High	High	Yes
Monastral green	Pottinger		Long	Zero	High	Yes
Monastral blue	Pottinger		Long	Zero	High	Yes
Ultramarine blue	Pottinger		Long	Zero	High	Nearly
Cobalt blue	Pottinger	Very	Short	Zero	Slight	
Alizarin crimson	Pottinger		Long	Zero	High	Yes
Burnt sienna	Pottinger	Partly	Medium	Slight	Medium	Slightly
Burnt umber	Pottinger	Yes	Long	High	Slight	
Raw sienna	Pottinger	Yes	Short	Slight	Slight	
Raw umber	Pottinger	Yes	Long	Very high	Slight	
Golden ochre	Pottinger	Partly	Short	Slight	Slight	Very slightly
Yellow ochre	Pottinger	Yes	Short	Slight	Slight	
Mixed black			Long	High	High	Yes
Indigo	Winsor & Newton		Long	Medium	High	Yes
Brown madder	Winsor & Newton		Long	Medium	High	Yes
Ivory and lamp black	Grumbacher		Long	High	Slight	

FIGURE 43. COLOR SWATCHES SHOWING VALUE RANGE.

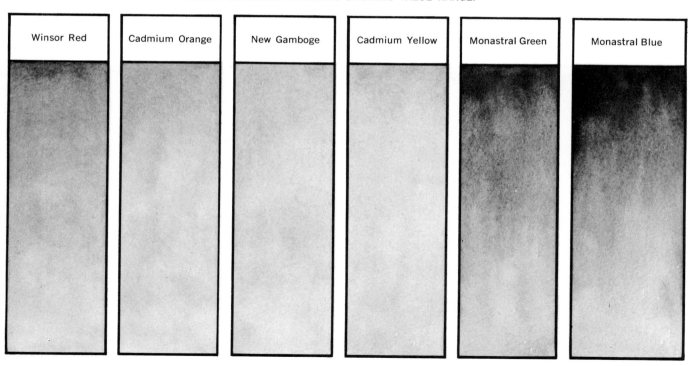

Winsor Red · Cadmium Orange · New Gamboge · Cadmium Yellow · Monastral Green · Monastral Blue

One of the best ways to understand pigments in combination is by making color wheels. Divide the circumference of a circle into 12 equal segments as shown in Figure 41. In the first wheel, we will use a triad composed of three transparent pigments, brown madder, new gamboge and indigo (Figure 41A). Brown madder is a low-intensity pigment or dull red-violet. Indigo is a low-intensity blue and new gamboge a bright yellow. As all other yellows are opaque, new gamboge is chosen despite its brilliance.

First put in the red-violet (brown madder) as intense as possible, next the yellow (new gamboge) and then the blue (indigo). Now the secondaries, orange, green and violet. Orange is made by combining new gamboge and brown madder, green by mixing new gamboge and indigo, violet by uniting indigo and brown madder. Next the tertiaries on the warm side of the wheel and red which are made with varying mixtures of brown madder and new gamboge; on the cool side by using new gamboge and indigo. Blue-violet is a mixture of brown madder and indigo with emphasis on indigo.

When the wheel is finished, note that the hues, though low in intensity, are unified and harmonious, with the possible exception of the yellow which seems to stand out from the others. This limited palette is an excellent one for rainy, foggy or dusty day interpretations or for low-intensity still life organizations. Harmony and variety are inherent within this pigment group and you will find when the three are used, that you will be able to paint freely and easily and in good watercolor style, for there will be no color discords to bother you. These pigments are at their best when mixed directly on the paper and are most luminous in the higher ranges of value.

The second wheel will be brighter, for a full-intensity triad is used (Figure 41B). Alizarin crimson is painted in the red-violet spot; new gamboge fills the yellow area and monastral blue goes in the blue corner. The secondaries—orange, green and violet—are combinations of red and yellow, yellow and blue, blue and red-violet, respectively. You will see when these are put in, that they are more brilliant than on the first wheel. The tertiaries and red are made by varying combinations of the same three pigments. Unity and harmony is inherent in this wheel also. The yellow doesn't seem to jump as much. This combination of pigments is an excellent selection when the intensity of light has increased. Try it for bright day interpretations.

On another wheel, try using Winsor red, new gamboge and Monastral blue. Winsor red is placed in the red spot and a primary triad is formed. This is a handsome and brilliant combination. If it seems too equally balanced, try still another in which you use Winsor red, new gamboge and indigo.

The large wheel is made for the purpose of study and reference rather than unity and harmony (Figure 41C). The basic brilliant pigments used in the watercolor box are related to the wheel that they may be more thoroughly examined and understood. The pigments chosen are, with the exception of cadmium orange and ultramarine blue, all transparent and are as nearly related to the spectrum as possible.

When painting this wheel, put in the primaries; first, Winsor red, new gamboge and Monastral blue; next the secondaries cadmium orange, Monastral green and violet. Violet is a combination of alizarin crimson and Monastral blue. Monastral blue is used rather than ultramarine as it is more transparent. The tertiaries follow, red-orange being a combination of Winsor red and cadmium orange, yellow-orange a mixture of new gamboge and orange. Yellow-green is a uniting of new gamboge and Monastral green. Blue-green is a mixture of Monastral green and Monastral blue. Pure ultramarine is our equivalent of blue-violet and alizarin crimson red-violet.

It is a good idea to tack the large wheel up in your studio and study it until you are completely familiar with the complementary relationships. Opposite hues on the wheel are complements. Orange is the complement of blue. Yellow complements violet, etc. In theory, when complements are combined, grays or black are produced. The most interesting grays are achieved by combining tertiary complements, yellow-green and red-violet, red-orange and blue-green, etc. The well-grounded watercolorist should know this wheel and complements thoroughly. Study along this line will pay real painting dividends.

The use of pigments singly creates brilliance, while mixing them lowers intensity. Limited and low-intensity palettes are chosen if one wishes to achieve color unity and harmony.

Now that we have experimented with pigments in combination, we will examine them from the standpoint of where to use them. Our selection of pigment must always be related to subject, light and expression. If one is interested in transparency and luminosity, both of the charts on pigments will be helpful. To understand the chart on "Pigments and Where to Use Them" (Figure 44), one must consider the notations in relation to these two factors in all areas of painting. Two of the pigments listed on the "Know Your Pigments" chart are not manufactured—mixed black and mixed green. A transparent black is a great asset, and a luminous one may be mixed with a palette knife by combining Pottinger's alizarin crimson and Monastral green in equal parts. Probably any other make will do just as well. This mixture produces a cold black similar to lamp black. If a little burnt sienna is added, a transparent black resembling ivory black can be made. Either or both can be used on a palette to advantage.

A beautiful way to handle transparent pigments is by glazing. When one begins to experiment in this field, unlimited varieties of luminous color combinations present themselves. The chart shown in Figure 45 indicates only a meager beginning in this direction. It would be well to begin on a heavy handmade sheet of watercolor paper, rather than on a student grade paper; the chart should be a valuable reference source and the heavier sheet will stand more handling.

The rectangles should be drawn at least an inch wide and an inch and a half long as illustrated in Figure 45. The easiest and most informative way of making this chart is to first paint all six rectangles under the letter R with a light wash of Winsor red. Next paint the six rectangles under O with a light wash of cadmium orange, or a combination of new gamboge and Winsor red to make orange. Following this, paint the six yellows with new gamboge and in turn the six greens, blues and violets. Use Monastral green and Monastral blue for the green and blue rectangles respectively and a combination of Monastral blue and alizarin crimson for the violet ones. When the rectangles are dry, glaze the top row marked R with Winsor red; then the second row marked O with orange and so on down to violet. If this procedure is

FIGURE 44. PIGMENTS AND WHERE TO USE THEM.

Pigments	Value Areas
Complementary mixtures, such as a mixture of red and green (These are black equivalents.)	Light value areas. (Values 0 to 2½.)
Precipitating pigments of low intensity that appear blackish in varying degrees: burnt sienna, raw sienna, burnt umber, raw umber, golden ochre, yellow ochre (Burnt umber and raw umber are the darkest of these pigments.)	Light value areas. (Values 0 to 2½ or 3.) The darker the pigment, the higher—that is, lighter—the value that should be held.
Mixed black Ivory and lamp black	Light value areas only. (Values 0 to 2½).
Low-intensity transparents, Brown madder, indigo	Light and middle value areas. (Values 0 to 6.)
High-intensity transparents: New gamboge, Monastral green, Monastral blue, alizarin crimson, ultramarine blue, Winsor red.	All value areas. (Values 0 to 9, depending on the value range of the pigment. To lower their value in low intensity, use brown, reds, blues, and violets and yellow where possible.)
High-intensity opaques: cadmium red, vermilion, cadmium orange, cadmium yellow, cobalt, lemon yellow.	Light value areas. (Values 0 to 2½ or 3, and for opaque overpainting in small areas.)

One should not use umber, raw umber, brown madder or indigo singly for darker values that is, below six, or get such values by complementary mixtures. All four of these pigments are blackish in character and raw umber is highly opaque. When these pigments or complementary mixtures are used to obtain values below 6, the darks are exceedingly muddy and lifeless. It is better to combine these pigments with corresponding brilliants having a long range of value such as Monastral blue, ultramarine or alizarin crimson to achieve this end. Dark values then have more resilience and do not lose their hue distinction.

followed, each pigment will be used in the underpainting and also in the over painting or glaze which makes the project highly informative. Note the difference between glazing yellow over red, and red over yellow. When the chart is finished, it should look like a set of jewel-like mosaics and it will if the whites are left exposed in the underpainting and bits of the underpainting are left unglazed.

It is well to remember that the most adaptable glazing pigments are the transparent ones. Obviously, if opaque pigments are used for glazing or underpainting, either or both of two things will probably occur. Either the underpainting will lift and combine with the overpainting, or the glaze will cover up the underpainting.

In either case the desired result will not be obtained. Glazes are generally used for light values ranging from 0+ to about 3 (as shown in the value chart, Figure 24). Below this range the transparent pigments are inclined to lift and a combination of pigments rather than a glaze occurs.

When alizarin crimson and Monastral green are combined, with emphasis on the Monastral, a rich, dark green results. Add new gamboge and the mixture lightens but still is a deep transparent yellow-green. If burnt sienna is added to the original mixture, one gets a dark olive green. These greens are useful, for Monastral green alone is a powerful, cold green and has a way of dominating green combinations.

There are as many different ideas regarding palettes and watercolor boxes as there are watercolorists, with each painter feeling that his own is the best. The palette illustrated in Figure 46 is made of 1/16-inch transparent plastic, and is 12½ inches long by 6½ inches wide. Half-inch plastic strips form the sides, one end, and the 20 compartments. The other end is left open to facilitate washing. The underside of the palette is painted white, leaving the smooth mixing surface as near the color of the paper as possible. This area will not discolor or rust, nor can the paint peel off as it is apt to do on a metal palette. It is easily repaired with a little Duco cement although it is practically indestructible.

Try always to use the finest pigment available. Inexpensive student paint is generally loaded with filler which reduces its strength and staining power; it is not a good economy. When pigment is set out on the palette, it should be pushed well back in the pockets and pressed tight to the sides of the compartments where it will

FIGURE 45. GLAZING CHART.

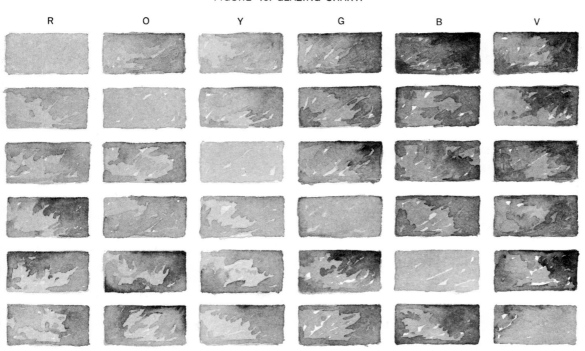

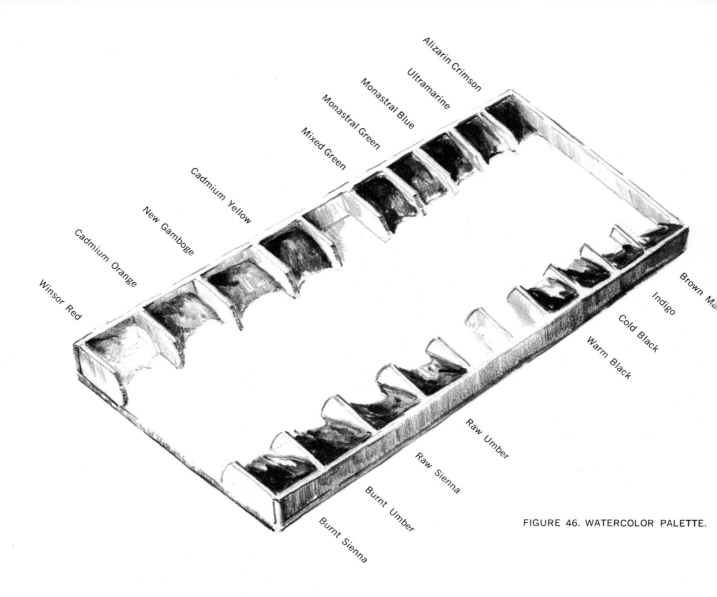

Alizarin Crimson
Ultramarine
Monastral Blue
Monastral Green
Mixed Green
Cadmium Yellow
New Gamboge
Cadmium Orange
Winsor Red
Brown M
Indigo
Cold Black
Warm Black
Raw Umber
Raw Sienna
Burnt Umber
Burnt Sienna

FIGURE 46. WATERCOLOR PALETTE.

not dry as rapidly since the air circulation is cut off. A wedge-shaped mound is convenient for lifting clean pigment directly from the stack. It also cleans and moistens easily when painting begins. If the surface of the pigment gets too hard to use, lift it out with a palette knife and turn it over; if it is hard all the way through, discard it. When it becomes crumbly, it has begun to disintegrate and is worthless. Loading your palette well is important; if the pigment is not on the palette it cannot possibly get on the paper. Put out plenty of the pigment that dries slowly. Pigments such as gamboge, Hooker's green and lemon yellow that harden rapidly, when exposed to the air, should be put out in more modest quantities, or at the beginning of each painting. Cadmium reds and vermilions have the peculiar quality of losing their brilliance soon after they are set out, and consequently should be used fresh from the tube. Cadmium orange is apt to be runny and it is a good idea to dam up its compartment with a piece of cardboard and let it set a while before using. A few pieces of moistened Kleenex laid on the mixing surface will keep pigments moist.

80

There are many ways of setting up a palette. The one shown in Figure 46 is arranged in spectrum sequence with the brilliants on one side and the corresponding low-intensity colors opposite. Any arrangement is acceptable as long as a convenient order is established.

The watercolor box that I use is divided into three compartments which adequately hold necessary articles, with space left over. A holder that prevents brushes from resting on their edges and getting out of shape was made by inserting a piece of rubber between two pieces of drilled wood, fastening them together and slitting the rubber. The box itself is held together by a leather thong, and when painted has a clean-cut tailored appearance.

Questions and Answers.

Q. Are there any other transparent yellows than new gamboge?
A. Yes. Gamboge, Indian yellow and aureolin are the ones most commonly used. All of them are more fugitive than new gamboge. Indian yellow or aureolin would make the best substitutes.

Q. Is there any substitute for indigo? You said that it was fugitive in high ranges of value.
A. Payne's gray could be used. It is permanent but not as transparent as indigo. Transparent black and ultramarine or Monastral blue could be mixed to make a transparent permanent pigment similar to indigo.

Q. Are there any books on the subject of pigments and their composition?
A. Informative and interesting literature on this subject is obtainable from Winsor & Newton. In it the composition of pigments is considered together with many fascinating, historical and geographical notations on the subject.

Q. Are Monastral blue and green the same as phthalocyanine blue and green?
A. Yes. Monastral is a trade name.

Q. Why not use other greens such as Hooker's, sap green or terra verte, etc., rather than mixing greens?
A. It is quite possible. Hooker's green is transparent and somewhat fugitive but it has the unfortunate quality of drying like rock. Sap green and terra verte are highly opaque.

Q. You indicated on the chart that cobalt was heaviest of all. Will you explain?
A. Cobalt is a true blue. Monastral blue is on the green side; ultramarine leans toward violet. The granule of cobalt is necessarily large for when it is finely ground, it loses brilliance; consequently it is highly opaque. The granule of cobalt is heavy and many English watercolorists use this characteristic feature to achieve an effect called "puddling out." This is accomplished by flowing a light cobalt wash over a rough paper. The grain settles in the depressions and produces an interesting texture.

Chapter 7

COLOR UNITY

The chapter on Pigments and Palettes dealt with color in relation to the pigment wheel; it is necessary to understand this wheel as it is the basis for the intelligent use of pigment. This chapter introduces us to color in relation to unity and harmony and is a big jump ahead so let us orient ourselves a bit before we begin.

The attempt to achieve unity and harmony is a basic human urge, and all life activity is directed, consciously or not, to this end. The methods used may be tremendously diversified but the objective is always the same. We can relate this idea to every occurrence in our daily lives and we will see how true it is. Painting is no different from any other life activity in that one's goal is the same—to create unity and harmony. The fact that each of us may go about achieving this goal in a different way does not change the principle.

As we think of color generally, we find that we are much more apt to use it for esthetic reasons than for reasons of utility. It is true, that wood and metal last longer if they are coated, but our main interest in painting the living room, for example, is one of harmony, rather than utility. We see this in our selection of drapes, chair coverings, rugs, even our clothing. Utility may play a small part but the most important factor in our choice of color is esthetic. We use color to help make our lives more unified and harmonious. The essential significance of color should be kept in mind. In painting, color need not be imitative of nature; however, unity and harmony of color throughout a painting should be the goal.

Color is not a vehicle by which an object can be very adequately described. If one were asked to explain a maple leaf by color alone, it would be impossible, since the leaf's color changes according to the changing seasons and light. The assignment would be much simpler with pencil and paper. A characteristic drawing of the leaf would define it. In painting, if form is adequately described by delineation, it is not imperative that color be used to double the explanation. When one sacrifices color harmony to achieve this unnecessary end, it is unfortunate.

To generalize, we might say that color should be used to satisfy our esthetic natures, and delineation to satisfy our rationality. This is correct as far as it goes but it doesn't go quite far enough. Color interpretation has a rational side also. For example, if you were painting a red barn which had a deep shadow cast on it from the overhang, and you painted the shadow dark green to unite this area with the surrounding foliage and so make it more harmonious, the general principle would not work. The green shadow might improve the painting esthetically but we know that shadows on red objects are red; in denying this, you would have broken the unity in the painting. On the other hand, if there were a blue bottle in a still life and you felt that your painting would be more harmonious if you painted it red, you would violate no principle by doing so. You would have simply changed the color of the bottle to create more unity and harmony in your painting. This is an oversimplification but basically it is the problem that has confronted interpretive painters throughout the centuries—how to keep a painting unified, harmonious and esthetically satisfying throughout, and still not lose the integrity of any object in it.

As we go on in our study of color unity, let us review the three dimensions of color—value, hue, and intensity—since we will be referring to them constantly. Value is the degree of lightness or darkness of a color. Related to pigment, this means the range from light to dark in any one pigment. Hue is the quality that distinguishes one color from another, red from orange, orange from yellow, and so forth. Intensity or chroma—two words meaning the same thing—is the degree of brilliance inherent in a hue. For example, cadmium orange is more brilliant than either burnt sienna or burnt umber, although all three are orange.

In order to reduce this problem to its simplest terms, suppose we conduct a series of exercises with watercolor, using a white cube or box. These experiments though concerned with small objects have a great bearing on landscape paintings generally and are particularly important when buildings are a consideration. The cube is placed in the sun, lighted on one side, shaded on the other, and then drawn in perspective, the close edge being about 6 inches high. Our color wheel and value card are close beside us. The first thing we note is the value change that occurs between the light side and the shadow side. As we look through our value card, we find that the light side is around 0 and the shaded side from 3½ at the close, shaded edge to 4 at the far end. Roughly, there are four changes in value from the lightest light to the darkest dark.

If we put a blue box beside the white one, we will see the same value change occurring between the light and shaded sides. If the light value on the blue box is 2, the shaded side will be 6. The change of 4 values on both objects must be consistent if unity of the object in light is to be achieved.

If we were to paint the white box with black pigment, the first step would be to indicate the light side, values 0 to 0+. When this area dried, the shaded side would

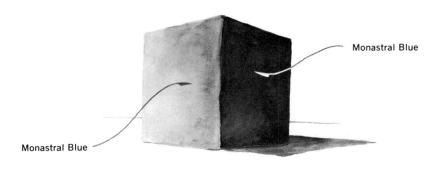

Monastral Blue

Monastral Blue

FIGURE 47. VALUE STRADDLE.

be painted 3½ to 4. In doing this we jump over or eliminate values 1, 2, and 3. This is referred to by painters as a "straddle." It is as though you put one finger on the value scale at 0+ and the other on 3½. The values between would be eliminated or straddled.

Let us suppose the box is blue. We loosen up the Monastral blue on our palettes and paint the light side of the box in a value of 2 to 2½. When this dries, the shaded side is indicated, using the same pigment. Monastral blue has a long value range and the required value of 6½ is easily obtained. In this manner the integrity of the hue is preserved, the desired value change established and a unified, harmonious result achieved (Figure 47).

Now, draw three more cubes and try the same experiment, using Monastral green, ultramarine blue and alizarin crimson. You will note by referring to the "Know your Pigments" chart that these pigments as well as Monastral blue are all transparent, have long value ranges and no black content. They are therefore well adapted to the watercolorist's use.

Try two more experiments using a combination of Monastral green and Monastral blue to produce blue-green and either Monastral blue or ultramarine blue with alizarin crimson to produce violet. When the experiment is finished, you will note that all the cubes are convincing in value, unified and harmonious in hue, and clean-cut and transparent in respect to watercolor.

Whenever a long value range pigment is used singly to achieve color unity in an object in light and shade, the procedure is referred to as a straddle by value. Painters of all times have used this method, which is often referred to as the traditional approach. When El Greco painted a blue drape, it was light blue on the light side and dark blue in shadow, a single blue being used in both areas. There is no better way to achieve unity of hue and at the same time preserve luminosity than this method. Unfortunately many of our pigments do not have the desirable qualities that the long value range transparent pigments have. Painting would be easier and watercolor fresher if they did. It is gratifying, however, to realize that half the hues on the wheel can be manipulated in this manner.

As all of our pigments do not have the desirable qualities inherent in the long value range transparent ones, it will be necessary to devise ways of satisfactorily handling the oranges, reds and yellows. Draw a few more boxes and we will begin with orange. Bright orange objects are light in value so the sunlit side will probably not be lower in value than 1. How now do we indicate the shadow side? We cannot use the same pigment singly since it has not sufficient value range to bring us down to value 4½ or 5 on the shaded side. If we use the complement, blue, to darken the orange, we will get a muddy, lifeless result, because cadmium orange is opaque and the complementary mixture will produce black. We might try adding burnt sienna to the orange, since this pigment is a dark orange and has a fairly long value range. However, it is also a little black and therefore not the perfect solution. Burnt umber, though also orange, and with a still longer value range, is also rejected because this pigment is even more blackish and opaque than burnt sienna. It is possible to move down the wheel from orange to red and on to red violet to achieve the desired result. Winsor red has a longer value range than orange and alizarin crimson still longer. Both pigments are transparent and contain no black so they are well suited to our purpose. There will be no trouble in achieving the value change. The difficulty lies in preserving unity of hue. After the shaded side is painted, glaze or rough brush a bit of Winsor red over the light side to tie the two areas together and also introduce a bit of cadmium orange into the Winsor red for the same reason (Figure 48). This will achieve a unified, harmonious and transparent result—one that is esthetically pleasing and reflects good watercolor quality.

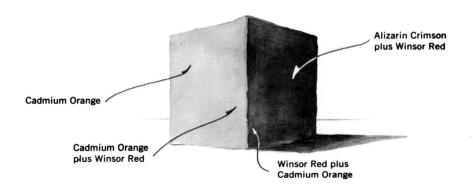

Cadmium Orange

Alizarin Crimson plus Winsor Red

Cadmium Orange plus Winsor Red

Winsor Red plus Cadmium Orange

FIGURE 48. HUE STRADDLE.

This method of moving down the wheel from orange to red to red violet is known as the hue straddle; it is actually more of a rhythm of hue than an actual straddle. When the Impressionists—Renoir, Monet, and others of this school—sought to convey a feeling of sunlight in their paintings, they found it necessary to use as much pure color as possible and often employed the hue straddle to achieve their ends. Their ways of manipulating pigment were different from the contemporary watercolorist's, but their discoveries contributed greatly to enlivening modern color. Our investigation of straddles is an attempt to cull the best from traditional painting methods and to combine this with the best from contemporary approaches—and, of course, to adapt these principles to watercolor.

New gamboge produces a luminous, transparent effect on the light side of the cube but it cannot be used singly to darken the shaded side. Complementary mixtures used to lower the value are unsatisfactory because they are not luminous. Using raw sienna, a low-intensity yellow, is hardly worthwhile since this pigment is not only opaque and slightly black but also has a short value range. Raw umber has sufficient range but is opaque and loaded with black. When we use the straddle by hue, that is, reaching away from yellow to either orange or yellow green, we find that neither pigment has sufficient value range, and if we go farther to red or green, the hue identity is broken. As we experiment with yellow, we are about forced to conclude that the best solution is to avoid painting a bright yellow object in sunlight. This is a limitation however that we do not like to fully accept. As a compromise, we will interpret the yellow object on the light side as either slightly yellow orange or yellow green. On the shaded side, use the straddle by hue. It will be possible now to reach a little deeper into red or to green to secure the proper value change without breaking the hue identity (Figure 49).

When objects are painted in a subdued light, that is, indoors or on a gray day, the problem of achieving unity and harmony is not as difficult, for frequently the value change from light to dark is not as great and the intensity is lower. Under such conditions an orange box might be painted with cadmium orange on the light side and burnt sienna on the dark side. New gamboge could be used to interpret yellow in a light area and raw sienna and raw umber for the dark area. When a bright pigment is used in the light areas and a dull one in the darks, one is using a method referred to as the intensity straddle (Figure 50).

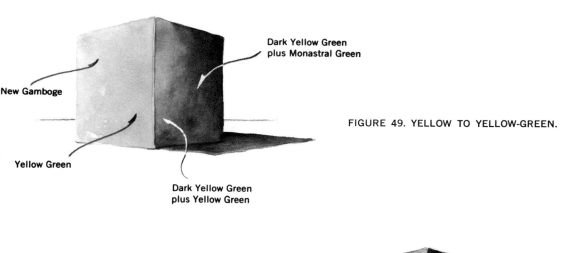

Dark Yellow Green
plus Monastral Green

New Gamboge

FIGURE 49. YELLOW TO YELLOW-GREEN.

Yellow Green

Dark Yellow Green
plus Yellow Green

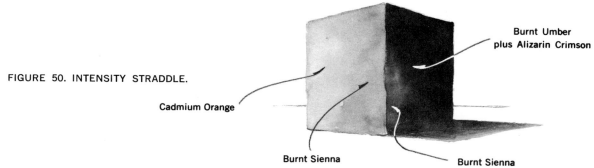

Burnt Umber
plus Alizarin Crimson

FIGURE 50. INTENSITY STRADDLE.

Cadmium Orange

Burnt Sienna

Burnt Sienna

In using this straddle, one should think again of the main objectives which are to achieve unity and harmony and at the same time keep the color passages fresh and as esthetically pleasing as possible. We might paint a yellow or orange box so that it was luminous on one side and dull on the other and even though it was unified in value and hue, it would not be esthetically pleasing, for the two sides would not be consistent. The next question then is shall we dull the luminous side or brighten the dull side? From the standpoint of fresh, live, transparent watercolor, it is better to brighten the dull side. To accomplish this, whenever burnt sienna or burnt umber is used on a shaded side, brighten it with Winsor red or alizarin crimson, even to the place where the brilliant pigment serves to achieve the desired value change and the low intensity ones hold the hue identity. If you are dealing with a yellow object and using raw sienna or raw umber on the shaded side, lean the light side slightly toward orange or green so that you will be able to use either a bright red or a bright green with the blackish, opaque raw umber.

The experiment with boxes may seem like child's play but if your objective is to achieve unity and harmony plus an esthetically pleasing watercolor quality, you will find the game exciting as well as highly informative.

Questions and Answers.

Q. If I were painting a box that was dull blue like indigo or Payne's gray, should these colors be used singly on the shaded side?

A. Let us suppose you decided to paint both the sunlit side of the box and the shaded side with indigo, which is possible for it has a long value range, the corresponding brilliant, ultramarine or Monastral blue, should be used on the shaded side to offset the dull quality of indigo. Indigo should hold the hue identity and the brilliant pigment should bring about the value change.

Q. If brown madder were used, would alizarin be the pigment to strengthen it?
A. Yes.

Q. Is it possible to get too much brilliance in both the light and dark areas?
A. Yes. Remember, however, that there are many neutralizing agents over which you have no control. Inside and artificial light, glass and the focal distance at which the painting must be seen are a few of them.

Q. You indicate that yellow is a very difficult hue to handle when painting an object in sunlight. Would you suggest eliminating yellow from the palette?
A. Certainly not. There are many other uses for yellow besides painting boxes in sunlight. This is like junking your car because you found a dent in a fender.

Q. What do you mean by local color?
A. Local color is the hue observed when the object is placed in a moderate light, say inside at a north window.

Chapter 8

COLOR UNITY AND LIGHT

RED HOUSE
Courtesy Mr. Raymond Burr

Through our experiments with pigments and straddles we have been attempting to achieve unity, harmony and a satisfactory watercolor quality in our painting. As we move on to a consideration of light, we should not lose track of these significant goals.

Let us begin with sunlight and observe how this sharp light affects the color of objects. Once these principles are understood, it will be easier to render objects under more subdued conditions.

There are five phases of light that influence color. The hue of the sky will alter the appearance of all objects that face it. The direct rays of the sun on an object will change its color. Shade and shadow areas occur when there is a relative absence of light. Similarly, deep darks occur when there is a more complete absence of light. To simplify our experiments we will refer to areas that are influenced by these five phases of light—whether full light or deep shadow—in the following manner:

A—Areas reflecting light from the sky
B—Areas in direct sunlight
C—Areas in shade
D—Areas in cast shadow
E—Under or inside dark areas.

We will begin again with a box or cube. Because our investigation now must be based on observation, it will be necessary to have a blue box. If you haven't one handy, attach some bright blue paper or material to a box with either scotch tape or thumb tacks. If paper is used, avoid the shiny type as this complicates matters. Only two sides and the top need to be covered. Put a piece of the same material underneath the box.

The box is placed in the sun, one side facing the light, the other in shadow. The cast shadow falls on the floor over the blue paper or cloth. Make a drawing similar to the previous ones, showing the top of the box. Our watercolors, value card and color wheel are at hand. The top of the box faces the sky as does the material on the floor. We will mark these areas A on the drawing. The front faces the sun and will be marked B. The shaded side is marked C; the cast shadow, D; and the under-dark, E. An arrow showing the direction of light is also indicated (Figure 51).

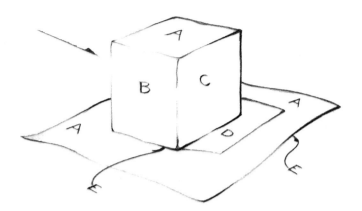

FIGURE 51. CUBE MARKED TO INDICATE LIGHT AND SHADOW.

Now let us make a few observations. On a bright, clear day, a blue reflection will be seen on all flat surfaces facing the sky. This light is most apparent up to ten o'clock in the morning and after four in the afternoon. Between these hours the strength of the overhead sun may overpower this reflection. This light is easily seen on flat pavements early in the morning. If the sky is blue, these surfaces will appear bluish. At noon, the pavement may appear lighter and warmer than it actually is. At sunset time, it will take on the predominant hue of the sky. As a puddle of water mirrors the sky, so does every other flat surface, although the color may not be as perceptible. Thus a painting usually will not be unified, unless the hue indicated in the sky is also introduced into the earth. The A area on the blue box that reflects light from the sky may be slightly lighter or darker in value than the side facing the sun. This is a variable, but if we were painting a number of boxes, the relationship should be consistently maintained. If not, the unity of all objects in light would be broken. As we look intently at the top of the box we see that there is a slight variation in value from the edge that is closest to the light to the edge farthest from the light. As we are interested in forcing the direction of light, we will overemphasize this factor. We also see that the top of the box looks a bit cooler than the front which seems to take on a warmer cast. In painting the box, we will use Monastral blue because this hue has a long value range and, as we have demonstrated, the value straddle is a good way to achieve unity, harmony, the required value change and desirable watercolor quality. Any modifications that we make must therefore be done subtly or we will lose more than we will gain. Monastral blue is the coolest blue in our watercolor box. Below Monastral blue on the color wheel is ultramarine, a blue warmed slightly on the alizarin crimson side. Above is blue-green, a blue warmed toward yellow. As we look at the wheel, we see that all the hues are warming away from blue toward yellow and orange and of course cooling away from yellow and orange toward blue. The simplest way to cool the top of the box and thus indicate the light reflected from the sky is to use pure Monastral blue (Figure 52). The area is moistened and the blue introduced near center. It is lightened toward the light by adding more water or lifting with the brush, and darkened slightly away from the light by adding more pigment.

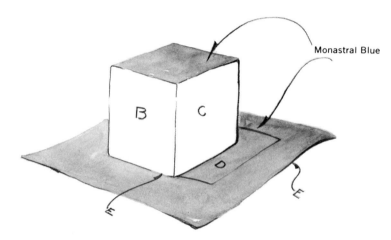

FIGURE 52. A AREA—REFLECTING LIGHT FROM THE SKY.

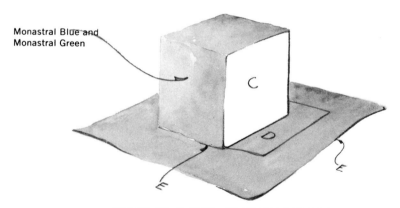

FIGURE 53. B AREA—IN DIRECT SUNLIGHT.

We now turn our attention to the front of the box—the area marked B that faces the sun (Figure 53). The hue of the sun is orange and all objects in direct sunlight are tempered by this color. They warm in hue so we should reach toward orange on the wheel. We can use either blue-violet (ultramarine) or blue-green; in either case we are progressing toward orange. My choice would be blue-green, for this hue seems more nearly related to Monastral blue and would be less apt to break the hue identity. Having no blue-green on the palette, Monastral green can be used. The B area is moistened and Monastral blue applied near the center and merged to the edges. A small amount of Monastral green is now combined with the blue, care being taken that this addition will not appear as a strong color deviation from the already painted A area. The surface is lightened toward the light and darkened away as with the top plane.

The next consideration is the C area or shaded side. This surface is darker than the other two sides because of the absence of light. You will note however as you examine the area closely that there is some variation in value. The surface may be a bit lighter toward the forward edge and slightly darker at the far corner. The reason for this is that the C area is one affected by reflected light which alters the values (Figure 54). If there were no reflected light, the surface would be a single dark value. It is interesting to understand why these slight value changes are seen. Reflected lights occur as light is bounced in from a sunlit spot. The shaded side must be facing the sunlit areas. Color is also reflected into shaded sides in the same way. The reason that the box is lighter in value at the close edge is that the shadow is shorter at this point, allowing light to reflect in. It is darker at the far end because the long shadow prevents the light from entering. The upper part of the C area is lighter, for being farther from the shadow, light can be reflected from the other side. Turn the box and let the shadow lengthen and watch the values shift. Now shorten the shadow and note the difference. Place a bright colored object parallel

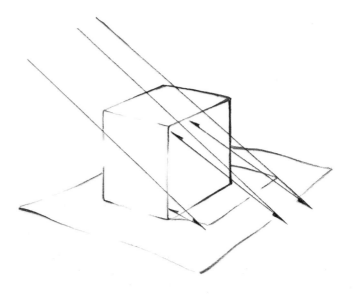

FIGURE 54. REFLECTED LIGHT.

to the shaded side and allow the sun to strike it and you will see the hue of the C area change. These experiments are fascinating but you should note above all that the reflected light is not altering the over-all value greatly, possibly half a degree but never to the point where the big change from the light to dark side is materially affected. The same is true with reflected color. It seldom changes the hue identity of the object in shadow to the point where the hue identity is destroyed. If it does, remember that unity is more important than a minor variation. Reflected lights are not found in B areas; the sun overpowers them.

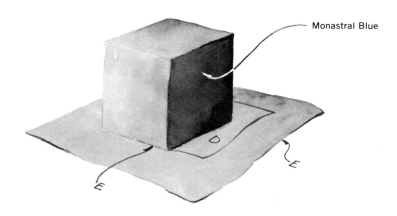

Monastral Blue

FIGURE 55. C AREA—IN SHADE.

In painting the C area, it is best to use pure Monastral blue to affect the value change and preserve the hue unity (Figure 55). The surface is moistened and the blue put in near center. As it is merged to the edges, more pigment may be added if necessary to secure the proper value. The pigment may also be lifted with the brush to account for the reflected lights. We will consider reflected color when we discuss white objects.

Cast shadows (D areas) are also caused by the absence or cutting off of light and are affected by reflected light and color (Figure 56). In painting, the cast shadow is used primarily as a means of explaining the surface upon which the shadow falls, rather than the object casting the shadow. A shadow falling on grass should be indicative of the hue and texture of the grass. Cloud shadows on mountains should explain the contours of the mountain rather than the clouds. Shadows should, of course, take on the hue of the object upon which they fall. If the hue and texture

Monastral Blue

FIGURE 56. D AREA—IN CAST SHADOW.

of this object are identical with that of the object casting the shadow, the value of the cast shadow will be darker than the shaded side of the object casting it. You will see that this is true as you compare the value of the C and D areas on your box. If the box is casting a shadow on the same material that you covered it with, it will be darker than the shaded side. If a cast shadow falls on a flat surface facing the sky, it will be cooler than one falling on a vertical surface facing a sunlit area; the sky influences the hue. The longer a shadow is, the more it tends to lighten and lose distinction at the far end, for more and more reflected light enters from the sky. The darkest and warmest spot in a cast shadow is nearest the object casting it, and the lightest spot is usually nearest the light. The cast shadow from your box looks lighter at the close edge because first light was bounced into the C area at the close corner of the box and this again was reflected in a modest way into the shadow at the same spot.

The edge of a cast shadow is most characteristic of the object casting it at its closest point of contact. When a bush casts a shadow on a walk, the shadow edge and shape is most characteristic of the bush at the spot closest to it. As the shadow falls away, the aspect changes; the light spots in the shadow become rounder, taking on the shape of the sun. These golden circles appear as elipses when seen in perspective. The dark edge line often seen where the cast shadow and light meet is an optical illusion. Check this with your value card. Shadows are not cast within shadows. One of the best ways to see the change in value that occurs in a cast shadow is by observing a parked car. When the car casts a long shadow on the pavement, it will be lighter and bluer at the far end; as it extends, it is more and more influenced by the blue sky. However, the shadow is dark and warm underneath the car, since there is little light and no blue sky influence.

In painting the D area, therefore, it is well to continue with Monastral blue, indicating this light about a value darker than the C area, as shown in Figure 56. Make the proper value adjustment as you did previously.

If you will now tip the box slightly or put a pebble under one corner, you will see that the dark under the box is very low in value, almost black. This is the E or under or inside dark area. It is seen under buildings, through open doorways, and windows that look into dark interiors, and also can be observed in cracks in rocks, deep furrowed bark and in innumerable other places. Caused by an almost complete absence of light and sky influence, this dark area is consequently always warm and low in value. A combination of burnt umber and alizarin crimson, with emphasis on the alizarin, is generally used in painting E areas (Figure 57). It is not necessary to indicate this area in a continuous line at the base of the box; a few short lines applied at corners with a pointed brush will do. The thing to avoid is a dark that looks black or bluish.

Alizarin Crimson plus Burnt Umber

FIGURE 57. E AREA—UNDER AND INSIDE DARKS.

Let us continue this experiment, using Monastral green, ultramarine blue and alizarin crimson as local color for the box. All of these pigments, having long value ranges, are adapted to the value straddle. It may not be necessary to cover the box in each instance, but if you can find some small objects that are similar to these hues to observe, it will be helpful. Remember, to cool a pigment, reach toward blue on the wheel and to warm a pigment, reach toward yellow or orange. To warm alizarin crimson, add Winsor red; to cool it, add ultramarine blue. To warm Monastral green, add new gamboge; to cool it, use Monastral blue, and so forth. When you have finished, compare the cubes with those done previously and see if they do not reflect more light quality as well as being unified, harmonious and luminous in watercolor quality.

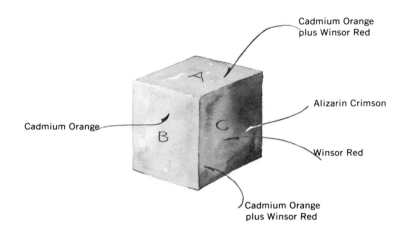

Cadmium Orange plus Winsor Red

Alizarin Crimson

Cadmium Orange

Winsor Red

Cadmium Orange plus Winsor Red

FIGURE 58. HUE STRADDLE.

We will now experiment with the hue straddle to achieve a greater feeling of light (Figure 58). This method of reaching down the wheel to achieve the desired end is generally done with pigments that have a short value range. We will begin with an orange box. As orange is the hue of the sun, it is best to use it in the B area. To cool the A area, we reach toward blue on the wheel and use Winsor red. To affect the value change on the shaded side, orange could be combined with Winsor red at the edge nearest the light and alizarin added at the far edge. The D area is indicated by using more alizarin than red, which will lower the value further and cool the area at the same time. The E area is put in as before, using burnt umber and alizarin crimson with emphasis on alizarin. When the painting is finished, if it does not seem unified in hue, glaze or rough brush a bit of Winsor red over the B area.

As we try the experiment with a red box, the A area could be painted with Winsor red singly or cooled by adding alizarin to the red, or the B area could be painted with Winsor red singly or warmed by adding orange to the red. Either of these methods can be used, but not both. The C and D areas are manipulated much as they were before and the E area treatment is the same.

When we come to a pure yellow object, we are again in trouble; while orange is the warmest hue in relation to sunlight, yellow is the warmest in relation to pigment. If we follow the procedure of tempering the yellow cube either toward yellow-orange or yellow-green as was suggested in Chapter 7, we will still have trouble on the yellow-orange side. If we paint the top of the box yellow, we will not cool it since this is the warmest hue of our pigments; and if we do not use yellow-orange in the B area, we will deny the hue of the sun. To avoid this difficulty, it seems best to go down the other side of the wheel, using yellow on the B surface and cooling the A area with yellow-green.

We now come to the intensity straddle which is especially important in painting landscape. This is the one in which a bright pigment is used for the light side of an object, and a dull one for shade and shadow. Where this straddle is used, compromises with what is optically apparent must frequently be made if unity, harmony and transparent watercolor quality are to be achieved. The reasons for such compromises are based in a seeming contradiction, for while light has no black, white or gray in its make-up, nature is replete with grayish and blackish objects. It is obvious, therefore, if unity, harmony and luminosity are the painter's objective, something must give.

We have not yet experimented with cylindrical objects, so let's look about for an old rusty tin can. On curved objects, the A area is not only seen on the top of the object if it has one, but also at the point where light and shadow meet. If the object is in light coming from either the left or right, the lightest area will be the point closest to you.

The can appears to be brown but this color definition will not do as there are many kinds of brown—yellow browns, orange browns, red-orange browns, red browns and even greenish and violet browns. We must first determine what kind of a brown we are considering in relation to the wheel if we are to go about this project intelligently. Let's say it is a red-orange brown. The can is obviously low in intensity and dark in value even on the light side. It would be possible to paint the light side with burnt sienna and burnt umber, for these pigments correspond to the local color. If we did, we could be forced to use black on the shaded side to offset the necessary value change. This, while achieving unity of hue, would not only produce a lifeless watercolor passage but would be a denial of light. The usual procedure, which applies to most all objects of low intensity and dark value, is to raise the value and brighten the intensity on the light side. In doing this, the hue identity of the object is held, the value change on the shaded side is achieved without resorting to black and the transparent watercolor quality is preserved.

When the drawing is finished, moisten the surface and introduce cadmium orange on the light side. Merge this lightly with Winsor red toward center and darken away from the light with more Winsor red. Orange indicates the light inside the can and is allowed to fuse with the red (Figure 59).

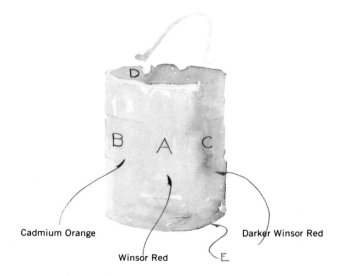

FIGURE 59. MODIFIED HUE AND INTENSITY STRADDLE—LIGHTS.

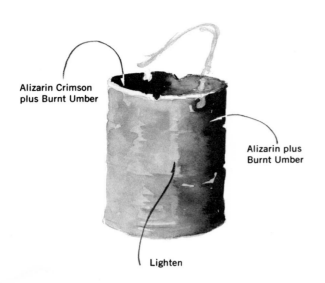

Alizarin Crimson
plus Burnt Umber

Alizarin plus
Burnt Umber

Lighten

FIGURE 60. MODIFIED HUE AND
INTENSITY STRADDLE—DARKS.

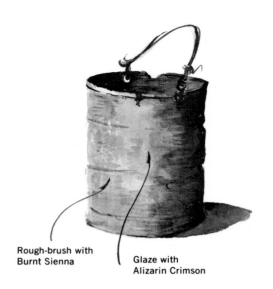

Rough-brush with
Burnt Sienna

Glaze with
Alizarin Crimson

FIGURE 61. MODIFIED HUE AND INTENSITY
STRADDLE—GLAZING THE LIGHT AREAS.

When the surface is dry, moisten the forward portion of the can slightly but not the inside. Use burnt umber and alizarin crimson with emphasis on alizarin at the dark edge and pull this combination together with the brush over the Winsor red until a gentle transition of value and hue is achieved between the light and dark sides (Figure 60). When the shine goes off the paper, lighten the areas with the brush as indicated in the drawing. When the area is dry, paint the inside. The D area will, of course, be darker than the shaded side.

To indicate the A area more significantly, glaze a bit of alizarin crimson over the central light area (Figure 61). The can may seem too bright and untextured to be characteristic of the object. If so, rough brush or glaze lightly with burnt sienna. The method we have used has been a combination of the hue and intensity straddles and is often effective when interpreting objects of low intensity and dark value. Make another drawing and try the intensity straddle alone and see if you agree.

Our next experiment involves white. This is an important one for nature is replete with white and near-white objects. It is obvious that we cannot paint the shaded side of an object with black for this would be contrary to both appearance and light. Most painters interpret this hue by using neutralized blue-violet. If the light is bright, the grayish violet will seem more intense, so Monastral or ultramarine blue could be tempered with alizarin crimson to get blue-violet, and the mixture grayed by adding new gamboge. If the light is less intense, a combination of indigo, brown madder and new gamboge can be used. To produce a neutralized blue-violet is simpler in theory than in application, for in mixing three primary pigments, we are apt to get muddy and grayed results.

Let us again face a white box and make a drawing of it. Paint the A area with Monastral blue, leaving white paper at the light edge and the B area with cadmium orange, leaving the paper white toward the light. The lighter in value the A and B areas are kept, the less difficulty we will have achieving the 3½ to 4 value change on the shaded side. The C area is moistened. Combine Monastral blue and alizarin together on the palette until a blue-violet that seems about right in value is secured.

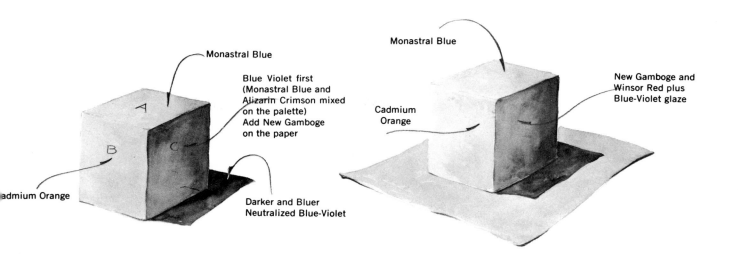

FIGURE 62. DIRECT APPROACH TO WHITE OBJECTS.

FIGURE 63. INDIRECT APPROACH TO WHITE OBJECTS—UNDERPAINTING AND GLAZING.

This is put into the center of the moistened area and moved out to the edges. Remember, it is inadvisable to combine more than two pigments together on the palette, so in compliance with this worthy rule, yellow (new gamboge) is added on the paper. This, of course, neutralizes and darkens the violet, sometimes too much and again not enough. It takes practice and you must expect a few failures. If there are reflected hues to be indicated in the C area—and white objects have a delightful way of picking them up—it becomes more complicated. Now we may have four or five combinations of pigment to adjust properly in value and hue rather than three. To do all this before the paper dries is a neat trick. Try first to get the proper value and hue relation with the neutralized blue-violet before you complicate matters with reflected color (Figure 62).

A second and often better approach to this problem when reflected color is involved, is to lightly paint the reflected hues on the C area first. If these hues are warm as they generally are, they will also serve to neutralize the blue-violet. When the area is dry, it is moistened again and blue-violet is painted over the surface. This pigment is lifted in spots with the brush, allowing the underpainting to glint through. When using this approach (Figure 63), only the transparent, staining pigments should be used for reflected lights. If cadmium orange, which is not in this category, were chosen, it would lift when the paper was moistened a second time and combine to make a muddy violet.

Experiment a few times with this underpainting and glazing method for it is one that is highly adaptable to landscape painting, especially when near-white objects are a consideration. Nature, incidentally, is as replete with such objects as it is with low intensity, dark ones, and it is a good idea to have some way of dealing with these problems. A near-white object does not have a distinct hue such as red, orange, yellow-green or violet, but is on the gray side with a tinge of hue. In analyzing such forms, first determine whether they are warm or cool, and then relate the particular warm or cool to the color wheel as we did with the tin can.

We will consider some landscape problems involving near-white objects in the question and answer section.

Questions and Answers.

Q. How would you paint a brick curb in sunlight?

A. All areas are light in value, not lower than 1½. The general hue, though grayish, seems on the warm side and in the yellow-orange, orange family. Reflected light from the sky and direct sunlight are indicated on curb and ground. Water is rough brushed over the area for it is good to let glints of white paper show as they add luminosity. A light tint of new gamboge and orange—in a value about 1—is applied to the curb and ground area and a bit of burnt sienna fused into the ground. When the paper is dry, the top of the curb is lightly glazed with Monastral blue. This will gray the yellow orange and cool the surface. The A surfaces on the ground are treated similarly either with a glaze of blue or rough brushing. When this is dry, rough-brushing may be added to the B areas if necessary, using either Monastral blue or burnt sienna.

Q. How would you paint the trunk of an aspen, sycamore, cottonwood or birch, in shade and shadow?

A. This is again the near-white problem, so first decide whether the trunk is warm or cool, and then locate the hue on the wheel. Rough brush the area as with the curb, allowing the A area to remain fairly dry. Apply a tint of the hue you have decided on, darkening it a bit in the C area. When this is dry, moisten the C area and add blue-violet, merge this over to the A area and blue the violet. Shadow areas should be completely covered with pigment. No flecks of white should appear here. Add blue violet to the B area away from the edge, if necessary. When the area is dry, paint the D area a darker blue-violet. The cast shadow should explain the rounded shape of the trunk and blend gently into the shaded side. If the trunk is too bland, glaze or rough brush with the original hue.

Q. How would you go about painting a cumulus cloud?

A. Clouds are near-white objects; all transitions from light to shade are soft transitions, for they are rounded forms. Moisten the cloud with the exception of the area nearest the light and introduce cadmium orange very lightly into the B area. Apply blue violet on the shaded side, lighter at the top of the cloud, darker at the base. Mix in new gamboge to neutralize the blue-violet except in the A area. Introduce whatever reflected color might be coming from the ground into the base of the cloud. Paint the sky last and indicate the characteristic edge. The top will be crisp while the base generally diffuses into the sky. Clouds cast shadows one on another but there are no under or inside darks.

A

B

D

E

FIGURE 64. CURB.

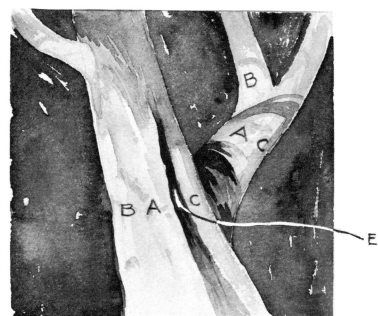

B

A C

B A C

E

FIGURE 65. SMOOTH TREE.

A

C

FIGURE 66. CUMULUS CLOUDS.

103

Cool

FIGURE 67. WINDOW WITH BROKEN PANES.

Warm Burnt Umber
plus Alizarin Crimson

Q. How would you indicate a window that had some broken panes?

A. The glass whether in light or shadow could be painted either light or dark blue, for this surface being on the outside would be affected by the hue of the sky. The inside dark areas would be warm for they are not influenced by the sky. Burnt umber and alizarin crimson are used for this.

Q. How would you paint a mass of rocks, stones and pebbles in bright sun and avoid being fussy?

A. This is the near-white problem again. Squint your eyes and reduce the B area to a common hue denominator. This might range from yellow to red-violet. Of course, these hues would be light in value and low in intensity. Rough brush the area with clean water and introduce the hues that you think are predominant. Remember that water is a neutralizing agent so the pigment may be applied brilliantly in light value. Flecks of white paper will be left exposed. Now treat the A area (Monastral blue) in the same manner and let this pigment fuse with the warms in spots. When the area dries, indicate rocks and stones with pencil, more by the way of what your painting suggests than in an attempt to copy each stone as you see it. Now indicate the C area (blue-violet). Where the rocks are angular, the edge must be sharp; where rounded, the shaded side should fuse gently into the A and B areas. Next come the D areas or cast shadows and finally the E areas to indicate a few cracks and under-darks.

Q. How would you suggest painting the trunk of a dark, rough tree, say a mesquite or willow?

A. The approach is similar to that used in painting the old tin can. When the deep grooves in the bark are indicated, which are E areas, they should be suggested on the shaded side only to avoid breaking the unity of form.

Q. The last two chapters have been concerned with straddles and lights. Is this directed primarily to still life painting or will it help us paint houses, barns, trees and water better?

A. The substance of these chapters is basic and applicable to both landscape and still life.

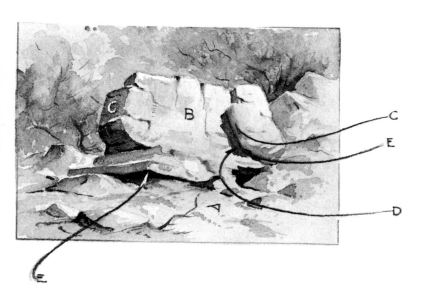

FIGURE 68. ROCKS IN BRIGHT SUN.

FIGURE 69. ROUGH TREE.

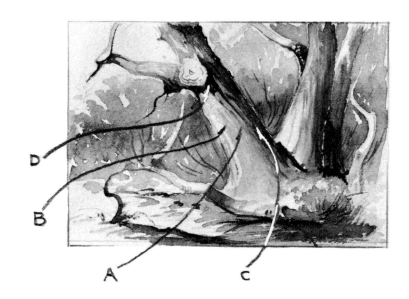

Chapter 9

A FIELD EXPERIMENT

If you leave the highways and wander off in the desert on one of the hundreds of little trails or roads, almost extinct from disuse, you will sooner or later come upon a ghost town. It may be only a few houses crumbling in the sun, or it may be a sizable village whose name stirs memories of frontier days—the Chisholm Trail, gold, silver, outlaws, gunfights or Indian wars.

South in Arizona lies the torpid little town of Pearce. It sleeps in a wide, hot valley, bounded on one side by a dry salt lake and on the other by the Dragoon mountains once used by the fearless Apache, Cochise and his followers, as a hideaway and stronghold. A dusty red road leads in, lined with fragments of old foundations and walls. Here is the general store with its false second story, empty now, but in its way still impressive. Houses and shacks, sagging walls, gaping doors, glassless windows, corrugated sheeting, gray wood, rusty pipes writhing from the ground like cobras lifting their heads to strike—all baking, sizzling and disintegrating in a gruelling sun.

There is a church in Pearce. A stocky little fellow almost spruce in the sharp light, it stands alone in a wide area, a fitting balance to the otherwise somber town. Its cocky bell-tower and rakish stove-pipe chimney cut quite a caper against the dusty sky. On one side the sun beats a bright, hot tune on the white wall, while on the other side, the cool, deep shadows glint enticingly with reflected lights. One knows that summer has arrived when the shade is more inviting than the sun. There is an air of excitement in the strong pattern of light and dark against the sky, and the little church looks fun to paint. Although this is a lesson designed to clarify some of the ideas of the two previous chapters, we might think of the church as a person, strong, solid and optimistic. This thought will add significance to our project and we might have a very expressive painting when we have finished. As we go along we will try to clarify as many procedures as possible.

As we study the church in an analytical manner, we see that basically it is nothing but two white boxes and that our previous experiments can be helpful here. The reflected lights are bright so we will use the underpainting method here to indicate the shade and shadow. If we do this, other parts of the painting should be glazed for this will help unify the whole work.

It should be stated that due to the limitations of color reproduction, some of the variations in hue, value and intensity to be discussed here are not evident in the reproduction of the finished painting on page 107; the reader may refer to the experiments in Chapter 9 for demonstrations.

A drawing is made and the A, B, C, D and E areas marked on the paper (Figure 70). If an HB pencil is used, the marks will erase when the painting is finished. It

FIGURES 70-71. CHURCH AT PEARCE—PRELIMINARY COLOR SKETCH AND FINISHED PAINTING.

is best here to go from the light values to the darks, so our first consideration is the sky. Though it is flecked with clouds and there are patches of blue showing, we will simplify this area. If we do not, the broken pattern will detract from the church, when it should serve as only an expressive foil and be in a way allied with the quiet, almost somber mood of the empty little town.

Moisten the sky area and float in new gamboge on the right side to darken it; lighten the pigment on the left. When the paper is dry, moisten it again and apply a thin glaze of Winsor red over the yellow. For a third time allow the paper to dry and then moisten it. Now, using indigo and rose madder combined, put in the light blue-violet clouds. Rose madder is used in this instance as it is a more delicate hue than alizarin and a good glazing pigment.

Leaving the paper white toward the light, we will use cadmium orange to suggest the direct sunlight on the front of the church exactly as we did with the white boxes, and Winsor red and cadmium orange to indicate the direct sunlight and the rust on the tin roof facing the sun. The warm gray of the door and the dusty window, both near-white surfaces, are obtained by first using a light wash of indigo and then glazing with orange. The old buildings are actually a burnt or raw umber. We will use burnt sienna brightened with orange to indicate these dull sunlit facades. The project is similar to that of painting the rusty tin can, as the buildings are of low intensity and value even on the light side, so both the value and intensity need to be raised.

The ground is a dull red-orange which should be brightened with Winsor red and later glazed with blue violet to make it lie flat. The bank at the side of the road, which is a B area, will remain untouched to amplify the sunlight on this surface. The problem is the same as with the curb (Figure 64). The road is much whiter than the earth and can be made to lie flat with the same blue violet used in the sky. In the close foreground, the direct sunlight is more intense. The bank is rounded by adding alizarin crimson to the top edge, thus cooling the bright red orange and turning the form.

Having painted the sky and all areas in light, with the exception of the trees, we move on to the shade and shadow areas. As noted before, the C and D areas are alive with color reflected from the ground. We will underpaint these areas, using Winsor red and new gamboge, as these two pigments are both transparent and staining and will give us a variety of yellow, red and orange. By using them, we avoid cadmium orange which is opaque and would not combine well with the over painting.

The shadow of the bell tower, being unaffected by ground reflections, is painted with indigo, the sky hue. When the paper is dry, the shaded sides of the church are moistened. These will be painted before the D areas as the shaded sides are lighter than the cast shadows. Indigo and rose madder are mixed on the palette and the blue violet is applied, the pigment being lifted with the brush to reveal the underpainting. The surfaces are darkened slightly away from the light. When these dry, the cast shadows are painted on the wall in a similar manner. Under the overhang of the roof, the value is darker and the hue warmer for here there is less sky influence. More rose madder or alizarin crimson should be added at these points. As the shadows extend down the wall they become lighter and bluer as the sky influence is felt. Indigo is therefore added and the edge lightened. Shade and shadow on the small buildings is indicated with burnt sienna and burnt umber with plenty of alizarin crimson mixed in. This is the modified intensity straddle as described in Chapter 8.

It is often well to paint the trunk and branches of a tree before indicating the foliage. This was done with both trees. One was yellow green on the light side with raw umber added for the shaded side. The tree on the left was painted in a similar manner, using a grayed violet to harmonize with the sky. For the foreground bushes and those near the church, a more intense yellow green was used on the light side, darkened with burnt sienna for the shaded side. As the door seemed to be more cool than warm, a neutralized blue was chosen for the cast shadow.

The under and inside dark areas are seen where the wall and overhang of the roof meet, under the bell tower and in the far window and open doorways of the houses. Burnt umber and alizarin with emphasis on alizarin was used for all of these.

We will finish our watercolor by adding a bit of hue and texture to the B area of the church to tie the light and shaded sides together. The ground is rough brushed in spots and a few small brush indications on the cross, chimney and small foreground branches complete the painting (Figure 71).

Questions and Answers.

Q. **You didn't say anything about the windows in the church. Why did you not indicate them in the first value considerations?**

A. It is difficult to determine the exact value of windows. They must simply be made to stay within the shadow area and should be done last.

Q. **When you glazed the sky with yellow and then red, why was it darkened to the right?**

A. To force the direction of light.

Q. **Why is it necessary to wait for drying periods in the sky glazes?**

A. If not, pigments will combine and luminosity will be lost.

Q. **How many times can an area be glazed?**

A. Glazes are most effective when only one overlay is made. They become relatively ineffectual below a value of 3½ or 4. If the value is high, three overlays are possible, but I would not suggest more than this.

Q. **Will you outline your procedure again in painting this watercolor?**

A. First, paint all areas in light and the sky. Second, all areas in shade and shadow. Unite the light and dark passages if the contrast is too great. Fourth, add rough brushing and finally, graphic indication with a pointed brush.

Q. **Do you always follow the same procedure?**

A. No. Every watercolor seems to call for a different approach depending on what one wishes to express. When brilliant light is a consideration, however, I frequently employ this method with variations.

Chapter 10

THREE PLANES OF LANDSCAPE

Villages in the Southwest have a character all their own. Unlike the cities which are young, vigorous, and unseasoned, they have more of the feeling of strong men in blue denims, rough, unshaven, a bit soiled. Gone are the days of the hitching post and spurs. Today the character of these villages seems typified by two neighbors discussing their problems from the seats of their respective tractors.

Hamlets reminiscent of frontier and General Grant days are peacefully settled in the shade of ancient pepper or cottonwood trees; the once active railroad station is no longer even a whistle stop. Dry washes, the desert and the relics of rusty cars creep to the doorsteps. On far-away roads, Indian villages melt into the soil. The heavy adobe walls house those who enjoy an endless, though dusty,

111

manana. Surrounding the scattered settlements, engulfing and dwarfing them, is the desert, serene, majestic, unending. On the highway one passes quickly through villages and towns and moves on again into the unchanging, mighty vastness. If one takes a little byroad from the main highway, it may dead-end near the side of a mountain where abandoned tools, heavy with rust, suggest that years ago some intrepid prospector toiled and failed. Here the desert whispers of its mystery, the saguaros murmur as the wind combs through their spines. One hears the turquoise calling of the quail, the strum of a flicker. The quivering silence is of an agelessness that invokes an inward stillness. A feeling of being the only person in the world sweeps over one. A feeling of being present in evolution sways one's mind, the evolution of a million years ago, that moment in time when the whole universe was still, that instant in time's span when an unbelievable peacefulness pervaded the world. For a moment Heaven encompasses the earth. The mountains lift, the haze rises. A shaft of light illumines the distant plane. It is the morning when the world began, changing but continuing changeless. Strange plants rear their heads—the ocotillo, cholla and prickly pear. A road runner cocks his head and tail simultaneously. It is a dream, a beautiful and haunting dream.

Back on the highway a car sounds its horn and one returns to reality with a start. He wonders if reality is on the highway, in the villages and cities, or if he has left it somehow back by the side of the mountain.

There is something in the spirit of landscape that is more important than a way to paint it; if the spirit of the earth, its people and its places is not felt, there is slight reason for painting. For one who loves the countryside and its people, this world exceeds a "one world" and becomes our world—beautiful wherever one finds it, wherever one paints it, wherever one loves it.

Though Arizona differs from Alaska in light, atmosphere and color, the fundamental principles of painting remain the same. They are not regional. So, regardless of where we paint, an understanding of these principles is necessary; it is only through such understanding that we can hope to express what we feel about our world.

Landscape exists in three planes—the sky (including the clouds), the distance, and the foreground. Within each of these planes are three more: the far, middle, and near sky. There is also the far, middle, and close distance, and a far, middle and close foreground, making twelve planes in all. Simplification is needed and can be done by eliminating the sky and distant planes. This happens automatically when one is painting in the deep woods or from an intimate subject. However, the foreground plane cannot be eliminated.

In order to simplify, it is necessary to understand the nature of all three planes. Let's select a very simple subject to study, blue sky with clouds, distant mountains and a sunlit foreground, and relate our findings to value, hue, intensity and form.

Let us imagine that the light value of the clouds is about 0+, and the blue of the sky is not darker than 3. The hue is cool, the intensity low in the clouds but fairly bright in the sky, especially the high sky. The cloud forms are rounded and soft with gentle value transitions between light and shade. There are a few crisp edges. The distant plane ranges in value from 1 to 6, the hues are warm in some areas and cool in others, the intensity is middle to low. The mountain forms against the sky have distinct edges. Even those that are in the far distance and light in value are not fuzzy at the edge. There is an angular distinction between shade and shadow in some areas of the mountain, especially near the top, while in the rolling foothills, the transitions are soft and diffused. In both instances, however, the value change from shade to shadow is close. In the foreground plane, values range from 0 to 9, hues from warm to cool, intensity from bright to dull. However, the feeling is one of warmth and brilliance. Form is revealed in an angular and linear way. There is a sharp contrast between light and dark. These observations, though generalized and not applicable to all landscape organizations or conditions of light and atmosphere,

	Value	Hue	Intensity	Form
Sky	0-3	Dominantly Cool	Low except Blue Sky	Dominantly Soft Rounded Blended
Distance	1-6	Cool and Warm	Middle to Low	Distinct Edges— Close Value Transitions
Foreground	0-9	Dominantly Warm	High and Low	Sharp Angular— Strong Value Contrasts

FIGURE 72. THREE PLANES OF LANDSCAPE.

at least afford us a starting place. They are summarized in Figure 72 for easy reference.

As we look again at nature, we note that the foreground plane appears to impinge on the distant plane, and the distant plane on the sky. Squinting our eyes, we see that these planes appear to recede in what we refer to as aerial perspective. It is light and atmosphere that cause the distant mountains to appear more rounded and bluer than the close ones. In fact, light and atmosphere alter the appearance of the form and the local color of all objects.

There is a rule of thumb which is worth while examining in relation to recession. It reads, "Objects in the distance are paler, bluer and less distinct; those in the foreground are warmer, darker and more distinct." "Paler and darker" refer to value; "bluer and warmer" refer to hue; and "distinct" refers to form. This is right as far as it goes. For our purposes we need to add to this generality as well as to the information on our chart (Figure 72), so that when various areas are painted, the values, hues, intensities and forms will be indicated correctly.

Low-intensity, high-value, cool colors recede more than bright-intensity, high-value, cool colors. For example, indigo, a low-intensity blue, will recede more readily than will ultramarine, a bright blue. We can say generally that any of the low-intensity pigments will recede better than the bright ones, especially in high value.

Yellow advances more readily than any other hue. The brighter the yellow, the more forward it will appear. Value and intensity being equal, raw umber, a dull yellow, will advance more than burnt umber, a dull orange. A bright yellow will advance more than bright violet. It is well to remember how yellow behaves optically. It should always be used lightly or in a neutralized way in distant areas because of its tendency to jump forward. Bright yellow used in the foreground, however, will bring this area closer than any other pigment.

Graphic suggestion, that is, in detail, also tends to come forward. This includes characteristic sharp edges, small brush delineation in dark value and rough-brushing. The coarser the rough-brushing and the larger the area, of course, the more forward it will be. To avoid having linear suggestion jump from its plane, keep the value and hue of the line used as close as possible to the value and hue of the painted area. Use light value lines in light areas and dark lines in dark areas. Avoid using dark indications in light areas.

Black and white also tend to advance. An angular dark will stay in the foreground more securely than a curved dark. One may put a dark, wedge-shaped cloud form in the sky and it seems to be just where it should. However, if the paper is turned upside down and looked at abstractly, one will find that the cloud isn't in the sky plane at all, but in the fore plane. It is a good idea to view one's watercolor in this upside-down manner during drying periods, for then the painting is seen abstractly and in relation to value, hue and form, rather than as groups of objects in various areas. An understanding of aerial perspective is necessary, if painted forms are to stay where they should. But if we hope to do interpretive, expressive landscape painting of any significance, the place to study is not from a book but from nature, for here are the real answers.

A landscape painting should not be thought of as a window opening out onto an unlimited vista, but rather as an open box with a closed end. I cannot emphasize this idea too strongly. It is on the principle of the hollowed cube that pictorial organization is built. Without this principle there can be no significant composition or movement. The sky or distant plane, if included in the painting, should be thought of as a "stop" plane—the end of the box, or the depth of the painting, if you choose. From this relatively distant limit the eye should return to the fore part of the painting. Otherwise, the picture will have no movement—either back and forth or circular. Consequently, it will be devoid of compositional integration. With the idea of the hollow cube and the "stop" plane in mind, examine Ernest Watson's *Composition in Landscape and Still Life,* published by Watson Guptil Publications, or *Cezanne's Composition* by Erle Loran, published by the University Press.

Nature is constantly changing. One of the greatest constants we have is change. We will never be able to paint fast enough to keep pace with the fluctuating aspects of light and color in the world around us. As we pointed out in our discussion of painting the church at Tubac, we should avoid unrelated values and shadow patterns. The changing aspect of light is confusing since our emotions rise and fall with the change. Expression then becomes uncertain, and selection and elimination random. For example, consider your own emotional reactions to a fluctuating day. When the mountains blend flatly into a clear sky and the foreground is sharply cut with darks, you are apt to feel one way. When clouds fill the sky and shadows dance over the mountains and foreground, another emotion is aroused. Later, when the mountain is a pattern of light and dark against a solid, somber sky, and massive shadows drift over the foreground, you will feel still another mood. We will devote more thought to emotional expression and nature in later chapters. At the moment we will examine ways of simplifying any of the landscape planes that we choose.

In the first place, before we can reduce the various planes in landscape to essentials, we should know what normally belongs in them. Our landscape chart (Figure 72) and observations will be a help here. Secondly, since art is communication, we must realize that there is a need to simplify. Watercolor is a language existing for the communication of ideas, experiences and emotions, and any statement made should be as clean-cut and concise as possible. One of the first responsibilities of the painter, therefore, is to determine what he is going to talk about. If he doesn't, no one is to blame but himself if he is not understood. If one paints all three planes of the landscape with equal interest, that is, with equal emphasis, a great deal may have been said about a number of things but the communication will be confusing. Study nature when you are not painting as well as when you are and you will see how interest shifts from one plane to another. Before beginning to paint out-of-doors, decide which of the three landscape planes interests you most, or will contribute most to the feeling you wish to express. If they are of equal interest, you will have to make a choice anyway. Next, decide whether the sky or distant plane or both could be subordinated. This might easily be possible if one were painting in the woods or along a stream. If you feel that all three planes should be indicated, decide which one will be your main area of interest. When this decision is reached, devise ways of subordinating the other two.

Paintings also should have a center of interest, that is, a spot where the eye lingers longer than in any other place. The first thing to decide, however, is in what plane one wishes the dominant statement of the painting to fall.

It seems logical that if the sky is to dominate, the largest area of the paper will be devoted to it. If the interest is to center in the distance, we assume that this will be the largest area, and similarly with the foreground. This is not always true, although such arrangements frequently lead to the most emphatic statements. In the accompanying illustrations (Figures 73 to 77), I have chosen to use the same simplified landscape arrangement to indicate how emphasis might be placed either in sky, distance or foreground.

In Figure 73 we see a type of landscape which I feel is pure corn. In no part of it is there a dominant interest; each plane—sky, distance and foreground—is given equal emphasis. It is unintegrated even in black and white, although nothing is suggested that could not have occurred here and there in the scene at a specific time. Try to visualize this rendition of the scene in full color, bright blue in the sky and strong yellow and orange in the foreground, and the disharmonious effect will be complete although a great deal may have been said ingeniously and honestly in every plane of the landscape. Not knowing where to go in the landscape, one decides just to go away. Unfortunately for the unwary painter, nature has a way of turning on such pyrotechnical displays frequently, and when she does, they are beautiful. But when the painter attempts to combine all these active and contradictory elements in a single picture the result is frightful.

In Figure 74 the sky and distant plane have been simplified, thereby focusing emphasis in the foreground. The mountain exists by implication but in its value relation it becomes part of the sky and so one might say the distant plane is compositionally eliminated. Sky and distance, simplified and united, become the "stop" plane. To achieve this effect, the value was kept in the light value range, not lowered below 2½ in either the sky or distant plane. The light side of the mountain was closely related in value to the light area in the sky, and the shaded side similar in value to the clouds. If color had been used to further unite and simplify the composition, the hue of the light side of the mountain would have been closely related to that of the sky, and the shaded side analogous with that of the clouds. Because the clouds are soft and rounded forms, the edge of the mountain was suggested as more

FIGURE 73. NO DOMINANT AREA.

rounded than it might actually appear. This further unified the mountain and the sky, and kept the edge harmonious to the sky, for curves are more closely related to soft transitions than angles. The shadow pattern on the mountain was allowed to merge gently with the far foreground. It would not be difficult with color to keep the intensity middle to low in the "stop" plane and still maintain transparency, the value being in the high range. Let us suppose that we paint the sky dull blue. Bright cools would be avoided. By referring to the chart (Figure 72), you will see that the sky was simplified by eliminating intensity, and the distance united with the sky by not including all the values that might possibly be indicated in this area. Actually, no violations of our chart have been made. It is simply a matter of what to use and where.

The foreground plane (Figure 74) was done in three areas, a close, middle and far, with interest centering in the middle area. The value range was from zero to nine, with the darks reserved for the close foreground. Had color been used, the foreground plane should have been kept in the same family with the sky and distant planes. If pattern is dependent on value contrast, it is not necessary to introduce opposing hues, since they tend to split the composition between warm and cool and add unnecessary eye attraction. If the stop plane had been warm, on the orange

FIGURE 74. EMPHASIS ON FOREGROUND.

side of the wheel, hue recession would then have moved down the wheel from yellow toward red. Yellow, bright or dull, would be reserved for the close foreground, yellow-orange for the middle area, reds and red-violets for the distance. Had cool dominated the sky and distant planes, hue recession would progress downward on the green side of the wheel, yellow-green being reserved for the close foreground, and blue-violet for the distance. Angular darks were used in the close foreground. The forms became more curved in the middle plane and fused in the distance.

In Figure 75, the distance is united with the foreground plane both being largely in the darker value range and the sky becomes the "stop" area. Clouds were introduced in this plane because of the size of the sky area. To keep rhythmic movement in the painting, the clouds were directed to the same two vanishing points used in establishing the foreground. The value of the light side of the mountain was closely allied to both the sky and light areas in the foreground; the dark side was related in value to the foreground darks. Thus the mountain plane is compositionally subordinated; it and the foreground patterns are considered and viewed as one.

FIGURE 75. EMPHASIS ON FOREGROUND AND MIDDLE PLANE.

The edge of the mountain was sharpened a bit, not only to bring the mountain closer but to ally it with the foreground angularity. If color had been used, it would follow closely the procedure in Figure 74.

Figure 76 focuses attention on the middle or mountain plane. Both the sky and foreground planes were simplified and quieted although the elements characteristic of these planes were not disregarded. In this illustration the mountain darks are allied with the sky which, of course, implies more distance. They could as readily have been related to the foreground, darker that is, if one chose to bring the mountain closer. This would be desirable if the mountain were larger. In either case the sky is considered as the "stop" plane. One should remember when using this arrangement in color that intensity of hue ordinarily does not belong in the distant plane. If, for example, the illumined side of the mountain were made too brilliant, it would take on the aspect of a bull's eye, destroying the picture rhythm and making the watercolor too sensational. This does not mean that the light value area needs to be drab or lacking in transparency; it might be thought of as a gem of light in a quiet setting, but not a neon light.

FIGURE 76. EMPHASIS ON MIDDLE PLANE.

FIGURE 77. EMPHASIS ON SKY PLANE.

In Figure 77 we see foreground and distance united, drawn together by an enveloping dark plane. This puts the emphasis in the sky plane, suggesting a sunset, though there are innumerable effects in nature having nothing to do with sunsets that have this basic tonal organization. They usually reflect force and vitality and are strong in pattern.

Let us digress for a moment and consider the way most watercolorists paint in the field. Because it is necessary to have the paper shaded while working and too few watercolorists are equipped with shade devices, they must sit with their backs to the sun and cast their own shadow on the paper. This is fine from the standpoint of shade on the paper, but when your back is to the sun your subject is getting it full in the face! There are few more difficult ways of painting a subject than that. Mountains, rocks, trees or houses present their most uninteresting aspects in a flat light. Light to the left or right that produces shade and shadow is much better. Try painting into the light for a while, even though this means getting a shade apparatus of some sort, and see how much stronger and well patterned your paintings become. Once you have tried, you may give up forever painting in a flat light.

Returning to Figure 77, although the foreground plane and distance are united, these two areas should not be interpreted as a single, flat mass; there should be a sense of recession through the close, middle and far foreground and into the close, middle and far distance. This is mainly achieved by values ranging from 7 to 9, and by modulating form and value, with the most distinct forms and darkest values in the foreground. If color were to be used, the bright intensity in the sky should not become a bull's eye, nor should the recessive planes in the sky—that is, those nearest the horizon—be overlooked. Generally the warmer, darker clouds will be overhead and the lighter clouds will be near the horizon. Although sunset skies are undoubtedly spectacular and colorful, the mood at this time of day is one of quiet and repose.

If you wish to experiment with the foregoing compositions in color, or better still, a subject of your own, I believe you will have a lot of fun and will gain some good practical experience. Work on quarter sheets of paper, that is, around 10¼ by 14½ inches. Do your watercolors in good technical style if you can, but don't let technique be your sole aim. If things do not go well with watercolor, don't hesitate to resort to tempera, overpaint or even go to your box of pastels. Push the planes around, being always aware of what is happening to you in a feeling way as you do so. Strike some intense pastel into a place where you think it belongs, and see if something within you says, "This is it." When you complete this technically unorthodox experiment, and the planes seem to stay where they belong, try the sketch again in watercolor on a half sheet and see if you can do it in an approved watercolor style.

As we have mentioned, the foreground plane is one that cannot be eliminated. More frequently then not, it is of dominant interest, and last but not least, it is usually troublesome to paint. I can hear some of my students say, "That is the understatement of the year!" But the foreground plane is forever with us. We may never learn to get along with it but we certainly cannot get along without it. Part of the trouble may be optical, for our tendency is to direct our attention to the sky and distant mountains. Seldom do we study the good earth so close to us. This is not all, for there are confusing elements both in drawing and painting foregrounds. The conscientious imitator will inevitably lose the painting here. Only as the painter realizes that foregrounds must be interpreted, not imitated, will he make progress.

Let us see what we can do to simplify a bit. The foreground plane, regardless of the number of objects cluttering it and the conflicting lines going in all directions, is still a plane. It may be flat or rolling but it is one that we are unavoidably looking down on. Even though we are painting a side hill, part of that hill will be below our eye level or horizon. First then, locate the horizon line. The foreground plane will almost invariably have to be done in three areas, the close, middle and far foreground, which for compositional and painting reasons are often interpreted as large, medium and small. These, of course, should be well-balanced as to shape and space, with the dividing lines integrated to the plane by way of perspective. That is why it is wise to locate the horizon at the start. When that is established, two properly placed vanishing points will help. Unfortunately, in nine cases out of ten, there will be nothing in the foreground to give a clue as to where the vanishing points should be. When one draws a building, the vanishing points can easily be found in nature, and the distances from the building then related to the drawing, but with fore-grounds this is seldom the case. They must often be approximated. The experience gained in drawing buildings to their existing vanishing points helps one know about how far out they should be fixed for foregrounds. If the ground is rolling or ditches and banks are involved, upper and lower vanishing points, if established, will help maintain the solidity of the earth.

All three foreground areas may be indicated as diminishing to two vanishing points; this tends to preserve the compositional units of the foreground as well as of the whole painting. Or more vanishing points may be used if necessary. When the foreground plane has been indicated and the solidity of the earth established, the next step is to pattern the three foreground areas. First the earth, then the growing things and objects on it. Here again, one is confronted with a tremendous variety—grasses, bushes, twigs, sticks, rocks, weeds, saguaros, prickly pear, ocotillo, ad infinitum. If one can curb his bargain instincts, even though everything is free, he will do better. Pick one motif, perhaps a franseria or burro weed. Note how it appears in the close foreground, distinct and separate from its companions. In the middle foreground, the single weeds form a broken pattern, with here and there a few stragglers in the group. In the far foreground no broken pattern is seen, simply a mass with a distinctive edge against light or dark. Now consider the larger creosote bush, desert broom or prickly pear. Note how distinct things are in the close foreground, how they pattern in the middle distance, and how indistinct objects become in the far area. Trees, saguaros and cholla, characteristic desert plants, knit the foreground and the middle plane together.

From experience I have found it better to repeat a few motifs in each of the foreground areas than to use a number of different ones in an unrelated manner. When an unusual shape is used by itself, it is an eye attractor and has a tendency to break the rhythm of pattern. If the same motif is carried into all three foreground areas, it is easier to decide what to do in each area in relation to value, hue, intensity and form.

The same laws of recession that operate in the three major landscape planes apply also to the smaller areas. Refer to the chart (Figure 72) and you will find that by simply substituting the words "close foreground, middle and far foreground" for "foreground, distance and sky," the general relations are the same.

In studying famous landscapes, you will find that the middle foreground is often the dominant area. Although when painting in the field, the close foreground generally begins less than 50 feet ahead of the painter, this plane is usually an interlude to the middle foreground, and should not unduly detract from the middle foreground. Or on the other hand, it should not be subdued to the point where it ceases to exist. It should simply be adjusted so that it fits but does not overpower the area of interest—the middle foreground.

Questions and Answers.

Q. Do you always subordinate the middle plane?

A. Unless it is to be the area of interest, either subordinate it or unite it with the sky or foreground plane.

Q. Would you be more specific about linear suggestion jumping from its plane?

A. Suppose you were putting lines on the side of a house to indicate boards or shingles. If dark lines were used on the light value area, they would not only jump into the close foreground because of their angularity and darkness, they would also split the simple mass into innumerable small shapes. It is better from the standpoint of recession and integration of form to keep the linear suggestion as closely related to the value and hue of the painted area as possible, both in light and shade.

Q. In Figure 75, if the mountains had been larger and the sky area smaller, would you have used clouds?

A. Probably not. A graded wash would have established the "stop" plane better.

Q. How then would you have carried the rhythmic movement into the sky?

A. By forcing the direction of light, that is, making the wash lighter toward the light, and darker away from the light.

Q. I like to paint sunsets and I think your suggestion of uniting the foreground and distant plane will help, but they change so fast I can't keep up with them. Have you any suggestions?

A. A sunset may be extremely exciting optically but unless great restraint is used, a painting of it may turn out to be completely corny. Whether the sky is turbulent and brilliant, or like grey velvet, the mood at sunset time is always one of quiet and repose. It is this mood we hope to reflect in our paintings. If you watch a sunset sky at one spot, east or west, north or south, you will see that the first light to appear in the sky is yellow. From here on there is a definite sequence. Yellow is followed by yellow-orange, orange, red-orange, red, red-violet, and finally violet, with each hue seeming to push the preceding one toward the zenith. At times a single hue will permeate the entire sky; at other times a greater variety of hues will be visible. The yellow in the sky combines with blue to form yellow-green, above this green, then blue-green, blue and in the high sky, blue-violet. This sequence may be so subtle it can hardly be seen, or it may be brilliant and clear. But the hue progression is always the same.

It is often possible to see every color in the spectrum in a sunset sky, but obviously all of them should not be recorded; once the rhythm is understood, any part can be used, as long as the sequence is correct. Knowing that this hue progression will occur, don't try to keep up with it, paint ahead of it. If the sky is in its yellow stage, paint it in its orange or orange-red phase, even though those hues have not yet appeared above the horizon. If it is red-orange, paint it red-violet. By the time you are ready to paint the clouds, the paper may be dry and the hues you have painted will have appeared. I like to moisten the paper after the sky area is dry before imposing the clouds, thus keeping the painting more translucent. Note how the gray sunset clouds complement the dominant hue of the sky.

For example, if the sky is dominantly orange, the clouds will be a gray composed of orange and blue; if it is dominantly red to red-violet, the gray will be a red-green combination. If this subtlety of gray is maintained, greater unity and repose will be reflected in the painting.

I seldom do any drawing prior to painting a sunset sky, but treat the whole paper as sky. The dominant hue permeates everything on the ground, and unites the whole scene in terms of hue. It is also advisable to do three sheets at the same time, trying to establish a definite but not too extensive hue relation on each sheet—possibly yellow, yellow-orange, yellow-green on the first one; orange, orange-red and red on the next and so on.

I hasten drying periods, if necessary, by keeping the car engine running and holding the paper over the fan. By the time the last sky sheet is painted, the first may be in proper shape to indicate the lower landscape. This may simply be a reference for the better one of the other two, which will be finished inside. The after-glow follows the same light progression as the sunset, but often moves more rapidly and should not be confused with the true sunset light.

Chapter 11

EXPRESSION

A rushing torrent of water excites us, and a marching procession of ants fills us with wonder.

Nature seems always to be tapping us on the shoulder and saying, "Look, this is wonderful! This is beautiful!" If we listen—listen with our eyes—something within us opens; perhaps, as Aldous Huxley says, "the door of perception swings." Whatever it is, we know that it is beyond our thinking minds, or even our awareness. As the door opens, we may see, if only for a moment, the essence of ourselves.

This morning I held a dove in my hands. It had flown against the window and was more shocked than hurt. As I held its shimmering softness of opalescent color, with its eyes black as burning midnight, I felt the frenzied beat of its tiny heart. The little creature in my hands was no longer merely a dove, but something warm, pulsating and unbelievably beautiful. I placed it gently on the ground, and after one graceful, swirling arc against the sky, it was gone. As a dove stirs a deep-set feeling within us, so a flower kindles our emotions, and the evening sky quiets and soothes us.

CHURCH NOCTURNE
Courtesy Mr. William Hopper

Two men walk along a wind-blown beach, one a contractor, the other a poet. The contractor, impressed by the miles of sand, wishes he had some on his lot. The poet is also impressed but he sees the whole universe reflected in a single grain.

From the tiniest buckwheat seed to the highest mountain, nature is the "Great Expresser," and as she is, it follows that she must also be the "Great Impresser." As artists, we can learn a great lesson from nature in this respect. If our paintings are expressive, there need be no worry about their being impressive. We cannot create as nature does for we do not have her creative tools at our command. All that she works with is objectively real—light, air, mountains, clouds, everything. We as painters must be content to create with symbols of these realities. As our emotions are stirred, so in turn comes our desire to express.

We feel naturally that watercolor painting is a high form of creative expression, and it is. But we should remember that it is a way, a means to an end and not a significant end in itself. If we become too impressed with the importance of the medium, we are apt to direct our attention solely to watercolor ways and disregard the most important factor of all, the end. If our aim is to achieve creative expression through watercolor, it is necessary that we understand not only the nature of our medium, but also the nature of creative expression.

To create means to make or bring into being. But there must first be an idea or an emotion. Creative expression, then, is the symbol of this idea or emotion. For example, if a man builds a chair there must first be an idea about the chair in his mind. When it is finished, the chair is the symbol of the builder's idea. The engineer does the same thing when he builds a bridge. The emotion is usually more important than the idea to the artist, although he too must follow the same pattern. No one has a corner on creativeness. It belongs to all of us—no matter what activity we are pursuing.

The many schools of painting in the world of art today, excellent as they are, can be most confusing. If one tries to cope with them all, while at the same time attempting to understand his own particular field of creative expression, he may run into difficulties. For this reason we have confined our efforts in this book to understanding one realm of painting, that of emotional expression, or simply expression.

Let us return to nature. No matter what or how we paint, it is impossible to disassociate ourselves from nature, for we are part of it. This does not mean that we must paint clouds, trees or landscape. It does mean, however, that regardless of how abstract or non-objective our paintings may be, they are unavoidably associated with life. For example a painter cannot put down a single hue that is not to be found some place in nature. Here in nature our emotions are stirred and the desire to express is aroused. Once this happens any number of ways of expression can be found.

Let us suppose that an expressionist is working with four other painters, a realist, an illustrator, an abstractionist, and a non-objective painter. Each would interpret the same subject in a different way—none of which would be right or wrong, but simply different. All ways are right if art is produced, and to close your eyes to another's way is only to deprive yourself of sharing in the world's visual enjoyment. Let us attempt to fully understand the nature of the field we are concerned with here—that of emotional expression.

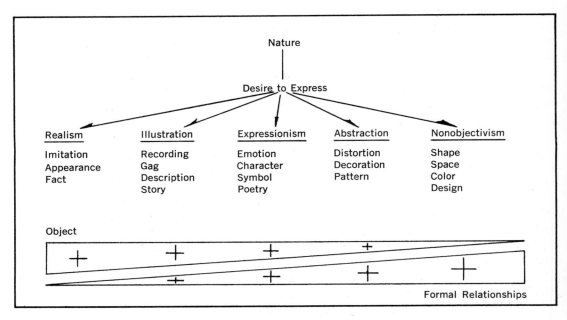

FIGURE 78. APPROACHES TO PAINTING.

From the accompanying diagram (Figure 78), we see that the expressionist is following a center or middle-of-the-road course. Illustrative influences are sometimes gathered from the left, and abstract ones from the right. With the realist, the object is primary, and relationships of color, form and line are secondary. In nonobjective painting the object is practically excluded and formal relationships take the center of the stage. However, the expressionist never abandons the object or reality completely though he may take liberties with his subject if he wishes; at one time the object may be more important than formal relationships, at another these relationships may play the dominant role.

Historically, the expressionistic way of painting—that of expressing feeling rather than formalized patterns—is the oldest in the world. Fra Angelico, Leonardo da Vinci, Rembrandt, Titian, Rubens, El Greco, Daumier, Degas, Hogarth, Van Gogh and Renoir, all in varying degrees, were primarily interested in expressing what they felt about the world in a poetic vein. Turner, an accomplished watercolorist, at times leaned strongly toward objective interpretation and at other times he emphasized relationships of light and merely suggested form. Always uppermost in his mind, however, was the idea of expressing in terms of light what he felt about the world around him.

Watercolor by its very nature is better suited to suggestive poetic expression than to extremely realistic interpretations. Similarly, as watercolor is not a tightly controlled medium, it is not particularly appropriate for mechanical abstractions which call for regimented space-filling exactitude. On the other hand, watercolor can be most effective for abstract emotional expression based more on intuition than on predetermined patterns.

When the artist paints expressively, the most significant factors he has to deal with are emotions, and how to interpret them adequately. The first step in this direction is, of course, learning how to paint, and continuing to learn. The second step is understanding the nature of emotions and how they can be expressed through the use of color, line and form. The more thoroughly these two steps are understood, the more significance one's creative expression will have.

As nature stirs his emotions, the artist feels impelled to do something about it. He is "stuck" with the emotion and only as he expresses it, will life return to normal for him. Line, form, value, hue and intensity are his tools, for he cannot work with the realities employed by nature, and must be content with these symbolic substitutes.

For reasons of convenience we will divide emotion into three general categories —those that lift us, those that depress us, and those that quiet us. The circle, shown in Figure 79, with divisions like the sections of an orange illustrates this idea. It would be fine if the painter could determine exactly where a particular emotion would lie on our chart—say two lines above static or four lines below. Unfortunately

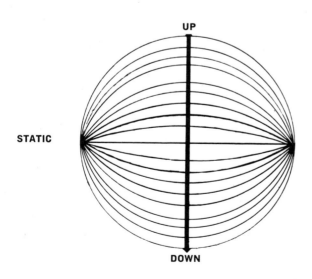

FIGURE 79. TYPES OF EMOTIONS.

this is not the case; our emotional and expressive mechanism does not work with such slide-rule precision.

Although the second diagram (Figure 80) is greatly simplified, it shows the relationship between emotions and line and form. In general, if one wishes to express a lifting emotion using a single line or form, the line or form should rise. If one wants to express a depressed emotion, the opposite would be true—the line or form should fall. Horizontal and near horizontal lines and forms express quiet emotions. You can substitute terms of your own for the various types of emotions named in

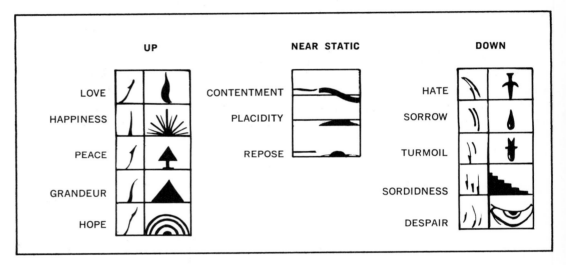

FIGURE 80. EMOTIONS RELATED TO LINE AND FORM

the diagram, but the relationship will still be the same. Oriental watercolorists well understood the emotional significance of line and form, and manipulated these factors with amazing skill in their brush drawings. With a single stroke one's emotions are made to rise and fall with the lifting and falling line of a willow tree, or are excited by the staccato shapes of bamboo leaves.

Value may also be related to emotion. Watercolors that are dominantly light reflect more emotional lift than those that are dominantly dark. Middle value is expressive of quiet moods. On the color wheel, the lifting colors are at the top, beginning with yellow, and the more somber ones are at the bottom, ending with violet. Similarly as the intensity of any hue is brightened, our emotions lift; as it is lowered, they fall.

An interesting experiment in relating value to emotion or mood is shown in Figures 81, 82, and 83. Select a simple subject and draw it identically with India ink on three sheets of paper. Impose a light wash on the first drawing, keeping the paper dominantly light. Drop to near middle value on the second, and to a dark value on the third and note the different moods reflected in the three.

130

FIGURE 81. LIGHT VALUE REFLECTS A LIFTING EXCITING EMOTION.

FIGURE 82. MIDDLE VALUE REFLECTS A QUIET MOOD.

FIGURE 83. DARK VALUE REFLECTS A SOMBER MOOD.

Emotion can also be classified as exciting and non-exciting. Both lifting and depressing emotions can be called either exciting or non-exciting. For example, a circus seen on a bright, clear day has an impact of excitement and lift, but a mountain viewed on a gray day enveloped in rising clouds and mist may generate an emotion that is lifting but not exciting. The same holds true with more somber emotions. A street, seen on a dark night, with a few dim lights glimmering here and there, may create an emotion of quiet mystery, but two cars colliding at an intersection will cause an emotion of grim excitement. Thus, the nature of emotions as they relate to significant expression must be carefully considered.

When a slightly curved line is used in a continuous flowing way, it indicates a sense of quiet. When the line is broken, angular and sharp, the feeling is one of excitement. A rounded form is less exciting than an angular sharp form. If value is evenly graded, that is, flowing in sequence from 1 to 2, 3 to 4, etc., it is non-exciting, but when it jumps from 0 to 6, 2 to 8, 1 to 7, it becomes exciting. Hue used rhythmically is less active than if it is used brokenly. For example, merging yellow to yellow-orange, then to orange and red-orange and on to red and red-violet creates a quieter effect than jumping from yellow to red-violet, yellow-orange to red, etc. This is also true with intensity. An even progression through the yellows from new gamboge, cadmium yellow, raw sienna to raw umber is less exciting than if the same pigments are used in broken sequence.

We must understand how line, form and the three dimensions of color relate to expressive painting—for these are the realities the painter must deal with. These relationships are shown schematically in Figure 84.

Dominance and balance are also important elements in expressive painting, as well as in pictorial organization. If one is interested in these factors related to pictorial organization, he may refer to *The Organization of Color,* by Richard Gordon Ellinger, published by Edwards Brothers, Inc., Ann Arbor, Michigan. Here we will consider dominance and balance from the standpoint of expression.

One may sit inside by the window on a quiet day and be thoroughly relaxed watching the distant mountains appear and disappear through the mist. There is a steady drum of rain on the roof, and the water moves silently down the window pane. The bushes reflect in little pools which the parched earth absorbs as though it had been thirsty for months. An aromatic fragrance from the creosote bush fills the air. The relaxing and soothing effect of such days is probably felt more keenly in the Southwest than in any other place for they are unusual here.

The dominant elements in nature that stir this quiet, but lifting emotion are moderately curved lines, rounded form, high to middle values, fairly low intensity, and hues on the cool side of the color wheel, ranging from yellow-green to blue-violet. If this emotion were to be expressed in watercolor, it would be necessary to

FIGURE 84. EXCITING AND NON-EXCITING EMOTIONS RELATED TO LINE, FORM AND VALUE.

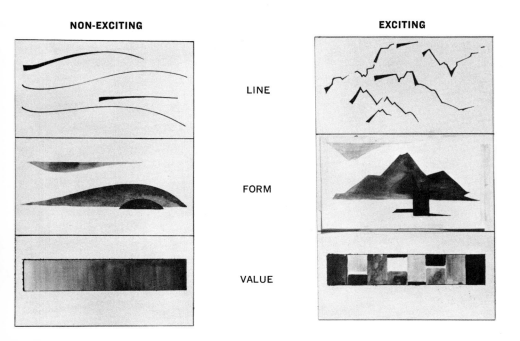

NON-EXCITING   LINE   EXCITING

FORM

VALUE

devote at least three-quarters of the paper to the elements in nature that aroused the emotion.

Let us look again at the view from the window. The darks on the wet trunk look darker than they would on a bright day, and the greens are more brilliant and seem to play in strong contrast to the cool gray tonality of the landscape. These are nature's balances. If they are neglected in painting, expression is not achieved. Nor can it be achieved if the dominance and balance is equal. In theory, the dominant element should be distributed over about three-fourths of the paper and about one-fourth of the paper area be given over to the contrasting or balancing element. For example, if the dominant element of a painting was in the light range of value, the balancing element of dark should be limited to about one-quarter or one-third of the paper area. If it goes up to a half, the painting will not be making an emphatic statement.

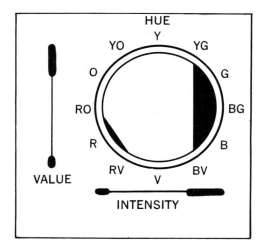

FIGURE 85. DIAGRAM OF DOMINANCES AND BALANCES.

However, in practice these hard and fast rules are not always applicable; sometimes as much as one-third, or as little as one-eighth can be used for balances. Diagramatically these relationships are often indicated by a vertical line representing the value scale, a circle representing the hue wheel, and a horizontal line representing the intensity range. For example, Figure 85 diagrams a painting that reflects the mood of our quiet day—it is dominantly light in value, low in intensity, and cool in hue.

If one were attempting to express the mood of a day like this, it would not be necessary to deviate from these essential elements of line, form, value, hue and intensity, for they all lead to non-exciting and lifting emotions. The painter would, therefore, accept what is given him and go on from there. It cannot be emphasized too greatly that the expressive painter is not concerned with the mountains, clouds, trees, bushes and water reflections per se, for objects themselves do not lead to expression. It is only as the relationships of line, form, value, hue and intensity are manipulated that expression is achieved.

Now, let us move to the desert with a group of painters. It is a hot day. The light is cutting. Sharp shadows are etched clearly on the mountains in deep blue-violet. The sky is a clear bright blue. Resting in pools of cool shadow, the close foliage is definitely green. Men perspire freely when painting on such days, and the ladies do a bit better than glow. When the paintings are finished, all go dripping back to their cars. Later when they re-assemble at the studio, the results, though technically good, are disappointing. Most of the paintings are predominantly blue, blue-violet and green, with only touches of warm here and there; they seem to reflect the Everglades, or the deep, cold North Atlantic rather than the desert. Their strong darks and angularity are not enough to give the feeling of the hot day or the sting of the sun. Remember, it is not necessarily what one sees, but what one feels, that will produce the desired expression when recorded. If one is hot as a tamale and wishes to interpret the way he feels about the day, he would paint the sky a dusty warm, not an iceberg blue, even though the casual bystander with a camera around his neck says, "I don't see it that way!" A hot desert landscape can be more significantly painted by changing the dominance of cool hue to warm. All other native factors would remain the same.

At this point an unfortunate misunderstanding may arise, for some will mistake liberty for license and say, "Here we go! Everything is fine as long as we express ourselves." Painting, I feel, should not be thought of as a way for the unleashed ego to go on a color binge. Personal expression should not be merely egocentric expression. True, expression *is* achieved only through individuality; but it must be something much more than an emotional explosion. The necessary control must be achieved through understanding.

The landscape artist painting expressively never loses his bond with nature. To violate the character of nature is an offense to him. To place things in planes of landscape where they do not belong is an affront to nature. He is not an imitator, an illustrator, an abstractionist or a non-objective painter; he is an expressionist who hopes to express the meanings that underlie and are reflected through appearances. One has only to look at the work of Constable, Turner, Homer or any of the great landscape painters to see how they felt about this matter. It is not necessary to violate painting or landscape principles or to disregard the character of nature to achieve expression.

There are two other factors that have much to do with expression; one is movement or rhythm and the other is shape. Painting is actually a static art form. It has no movement of its own as has music, the theater, or the dance. Even literature has more movement than painting—the mind moves in sequence from one idea to the next until it reaches the end. On the other hand, sculpture and architecture are static art forms similar to painting.

Movement in painting is achieved only as the viewer's eye is directed through the pictorial organization. The painting doesn't move; the eye does. If the eye is directed through the painting rapidly or in a staccato manner, the expression is one of excitement. If the movement is slower, the effect is less exciting. It is evident that what is referred to as the path of the eye in pictorial organization is important expressively. For the reader who wishes to pursue this subject further, I strongly recommend the two previously mentioned books on composition by Watson and Loran.

The shape one selects for his painting has much to do with expression, for a shape is expressive in itself. The artist who always works on the same-sized paper loses an advantage which could so easily be his. A basic principle of Dynamic Symmetry can be most useful here. For example, a sturdy, handsome piece of architecture might seem well adapted to a square, while a long, sweeping landscape would probably be better in root three or four than it would be in root two. In painting, if one feels an emotion in relation to a good dynamic shape, composition as well as feeling can be more readily expressed. The diagram (Figure 86) indicates the way in which the various roots are derived, and is convenient to use when making dummies. The reciprocals are given to facilitate cutting paper to the desired proportion.

FIGURE 86. METHOD OF ESTABLISHING DYNAMIC SHAPES.

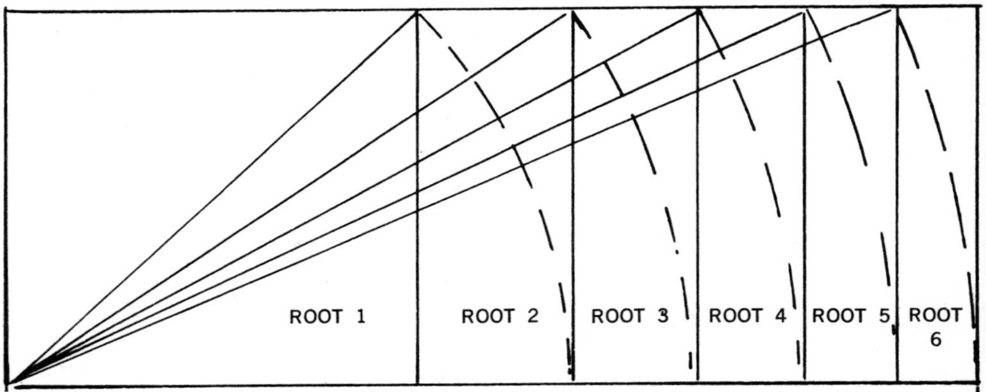

RECIPROCALS		
ROOT 1	1	DIVIDE LENGTH BY RECIPROCAL
ROOT 2	1.41	TO GET WIDTH—
ROOT 3	1.73	MULTIPLY WIDTH BY RECIPROCAL
ROOT 4	2	TO GET LENGTH
ROOT 5	2.24	
ROOT 6	2.45	

Questions and Answers.

Q. How would you define nature?

A. According to Webster it is the existing condition of things, and this definition seems broad enough. As long as we don't confine nature to something outside the window, or separate ourselves from it, or feel that it does not exist within us as well as outside us, it seems to me that we are on the right track.

Q. Do you think that anyone fully understands the feeling an artist wishes to convey?

A. Probably not, for each person's interpretation of a painting must be different. It doesn't matter too much as long as the main emotional impact of the painting communicates.

Q. Why do you feel that middle value should be avoided in watercolor?

A. This question has been taken up before, but perhaps could be expanded. Watercolor at its best should be clear and transparent in the light values and rich and resilient in the darks. When a painting is organized with the middle values dominant these qualities are hard to achieve. Furthermore, middle value dominance calls for a double balance of both light and dark which is technically difficult to achieve. The easiest way out of this dilemma is to avoid middle value organizations.

Q. Would you really take a group of students out on the desert on a day such as you described, and ask them to paint a blue sky a dusty warm and then make all the necessary adjustments throughout the painting that this deviation from nature would call for?

A. I certainly would not attempt such a project with a beginning group. However, with an advanced group of students it would be creatively exciting. If the group were only reasonably good painters, we would probably do the landscape fairly literally in the field, then analyze the paintings in the studio from the standpoint of expression. Then we would try it again out-of-doors.

Q. Do you ever do abstract or non-objective paintings?

A. Yes, also collages.

Q. Why?

A. Because they are fun and help contribute to more expressive landscape painting.

Q. Do you ever teach these subjects?

A. No. There are others better qualified.

Q. Do you usually work on exact dynamic shapes?

A. Yes. I feel that shapes that are not one thing or another are the most difficult to organize compositionally.

Q. If a watercolor is not successful in its entirety, why not put a mat around it, cutting off the edges?

A. Don't get in the habit of matting things down. Soon you will start with a full sheet and end up with a postage stamp. Learn to compose the whole area you are working on.

Chapter 12

PERCEPTION

CATHEDRAL INTERIOR
Courtesy Mrs. M. D. Judd

South of the border stands a church, its ruins reminiscent of the austere grandeur that once was Spain's Mexico. Old and abandoned, its handsome stone facade has been removed, and like a polished death mask, adorns the wall of a university building. Along the edge of its sturdy abutments a stream moves silently through the quiet valley. Moss-covered bridges span the brook which once, roaring with a mighty vengeance, helped smelt ore that flowed from the fabulous mines of Guanaguato. Burros wander up and down the dusty path as they have for generations. Turret walls, covered with vines, rise above the trees. These are the last monuments of a rich, proud city, the echo of yesterday's might and splendor.

The church is doorless, the dusty floor pockmarked with little craters. Here the ant lions build their homes and set their traps. The altar is gone except for a pile of crumbling masonry, and no figures mark the Stations of the Cross. Classic pilasters and the tarnished glint of gold and blue mark a period of restoration when the Grecian sweep softened and weakened the austerity of the Spanish line. To the left are the cloisters where the padres lived and walked. Here are the remnants of the old kitchen. Swallows sweep like ghosts through the high windows to nest in the dark tower and dome.

Painting in the gray stillness, every care in my mind seems to dissipate, as here, in the shadows of yesterday, time ceases to be. Eternity is now. . . . Silently, three little Mexican boys make their way to the altar. Their bare feet stir the dust, which in turn spins halos in the light. Gently they lay a heaping armful of wild flowers on the rough stones before the altar, and as quietly as they have come, they depart.

Probably one of the first obligations of a teacher is to be explicit—to say what he means clearly, simply and understandably. But I wonder if this is always possible. It is possible to show students how to do a graded wash or how to make one area in a painting rich and vibrant, another quiet and subdued. But if one tried to explain this church, inch by inch and stone by stone, it would dissolve into nothingness. There are things that are scientifically real and those that exist by perception. One is as real as another. They are simply different kinds of reality. One is based on fact—inches and yards, weights and materials, the number of stones, the amount of water, the kind of pigment; the other on an inner knowing, an awareness that is as clearly felt as though a voice had spoken. This is perception. The mysteries of life can be as perceptively real as fact is scientifically real. But they cannot be logically explained—like a mystery story that unfolds to a conclusion. Real mysteries can never be explained. They remain mysteries forever.

I painted the interior of the Spanish church many times and in many ways in an effort to express something I felt perceptively—something that defied rational explanation. I made probing, analytical drawings in an attempt to discover its underlying character; I tried different approaches and experimented with varying relations of light, on location and in my studio. Finally after ten unsuccessful attempts, the papers were put away. The watercolors were successful technically but they simply did not say anything! They reminded me of the story of the famous comedian who, one evening, was unable to appear. His place was taken by his understudy, who went through the lines and gestures with complete fidelity. He was exactly like the master with one exception. He wasn't funny.

A year or so later I was following a trail beside a quiet lake in another part of the world, and the memory of the church came back to me. I saw the path with the burros, the old ruins, the bridges and the gray, cool interior, and something within me said, "It wasn't gray, it wasn't blue. It wasn't a dull orange tinted with the gold of the frescoes, or the hue of the dusty floor. It was green, a yellow-green merging to blue-green."

"Nonsense," I said. "There wasn't a touch of green or blue-green anywhere, and anyway, this was inside and inside darks must be warm because there is no reflection from the sky."

"Try it," the voice said.

"Ridiculous," I continued. "There was nothing there to imply such a relationship. It won't work." But I tried it.

Following the usual procedure, the drawing was done first; then the light values building up to the final darks in a hue relation that ran from yellow-green to blue-green balanced on warm grays. The hue relations bounced back despite my rational observations to the contrary, and again something within me said, "Yes, yes, this is it." When the painting was finished, the architecture seemed unfortunately stiff as though it had been fitted together piece by piece like a jig saw puzzle. It didn't convey the feeling of a unit. It was solid enough—too solid, in fact.

"Let it grow up. Let it evolve," the voice said. "That's the way it began. That's what it is still doing. Evolution is a reality."

On another piece of paper the same hue relation was flowed over the whole sheet, darker toward the edges, lighter near center. The pigment ran and fused together. It was exciting as at last I knew I was on the right track. The value was carried down to nearly 4, with the lights around 0 to 1. When the paper dried, some loose, suggestive drawing was introduced, and the paper lightly moistened again. As the dark values were painted, the form was pulled out of the color mass. Strange shapes appeared. A figure in a niche suggested itself, light filtered in from the upper window. The painting was evolving; it was growing. I was no longer telling it. It was telling me.

When the painting was finished, it was not a replica of the place in either form or color but it seemed perceptively real to me. Again I could feel that cool, gray interior, hear the murmur of the brook, see the burros and the ruins, and the little bare-foot boys carrying flowers to the dusty altar.

When you paint perceptively, I feel that you graduate from the status of a painter to that of an artist. This is not easy; as thinking people, we are in the habit of turning to our minds to solve our problems. However, if perception is to have dominion, the mind must be stilled. There can be no turning to the mind for answers when difficulties arise; no asking what value is called for here or what hue should be used there. The mind of the highly skilled creative artist is like a beautifully balanced and keenly sharpened tool that is placed unreservedly in the hands of perception.

You do not have to wait until you are a finished technician to paint perceptively. This is a little like stocking the deep freeze, just in case, but never using the food. A single principle learned well and turned over to one's perceptive mind to use is better than 100 principles that are never used creatively.

Let's try it. Begin with color, letting it flow lightly and fuse, or treat it in a more angular way suggestive of abstract forms or non-objective patterns. Before objects are definitely indicated, you may decide to use the paper vertically rather than horizontally, or vice versa. Perhaps you will not paint from objects or a landscape but will simply let the color forms suggest your subject—a bottle, tree, mountain,

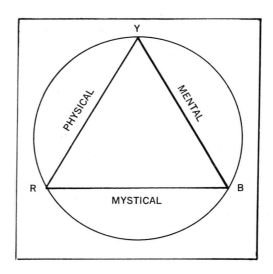

FIGURE 87. THREE CATEGORIES OF COLOR.

castle, or a quiet forest pool. From there let your imagination continue to evolve. You will find it creatively exciting—and great fun in the bargain!

We have considered color in relation to light and pigment but there are other interesting ways of looking at it. For example the color wheel may be divided into three categories as shown in Figure 87. In this scheme hues ranging from yellow-orange to red may be thought of as physical, the ones from yellow to blue-green, mental, and those from blue to red-violet, spiritual or mystical. The physical hues reflect energy and vitality, the most dynamic of all being orange. If one visualizes a sunlit room painted in bright orange, he will realize that the impact is too violent. A clear, bright yellow is exciting but more mentally so than physically. In the Orient, yellow is often considered to be a spiritual hue. The low-intensity yellow-greens and blue-greens frequently used in libraries and studies are conducive to thought and relaxation. The mystical hues, beginning with blue and ending with red-violet, for centuries have been associated with spiritual values and royalty.

As we understand these three divisions of color and are able to associate them with emotion, expressive painting will become simplified for us. We see color with our eyes in one way, but we may feel perceptively about it in quite a different way. When the group of painters mentioned in Chapter 11 tried to interpret a hot day, it was difficult for some of them to do so through the use of cool hues. They were impelled to use warms that were more reflective of the energy and vitality of the day as they felt it. Others painted the landscape as they saw it. Here we have two ways, neither of them right or wrong, but simply different. If, however, one has a feeling for the three categories of color, he should capitalize on it.

It often is not the lack of awareness or perception that accounts for a painter's inability to express what he feels, but rather a lack of understanding of the principles that must be used to achieve this expression. It seems to take a long time to

DESERT STORM

realize that, in addition to our subject, our symbols of expression—line, form, value, hue, intensity, movement and shape—are of major importance. The more fully you understand these principles, the more expressively satisfying your paintings will be.

A fine spring morning arrives. The air is soft and gentle. Everything is clean, the earth is newly born. Gossamer leaves film the bare winter branches. The hills melt into the moist sky. Each jewel-studded blade of grass twinkles in the sun. You say, "Certainly this can be done in watercolor. It is light and wet, clean, transparent, suggestive. The medium is ideally suited to express exactly what I feel." And it is, if you understand. . . . Night comes and you wander down a quiet street. The houses melt into the rich, dark sky, the tree masses soften and disappear. Figures glide in and out of the shadows, revealed for a moment and then are lost. Can this be done in watercolor? Can this mood be reflected? It can, if you go about it properly.

Nature is replete with mysteries—the arrival of spring, the awakening of life, the coming of night. True mysteries cannot be explained scientifically or analytically. But the purpose of painting is not the same as that of scientific explanation. Rather, it is to say—as best we can—that which is unsayable.

The expression of mystery is based on suggestion. This necessitates a knowledge of the principle of emphasis and subordination, and the more clearly this principle is understood, the more vitality your statement will have. The six sketches shown in Figure 88 (see facing page) will serve to illustrate the principle. In the first sketch, a simple white shape drawn against a white background, the light side of the object is lost or subordinated in the background. The dark or shaded side is all that can be seen. If the object is placed in front of a gray background, as in the second sketch, the lights and darks will be seen, but the values that correspond to the background will be lost. A background that is the same value as the darks, will throw emphasis on the lights, and the shaded side will be lost, as in the third sketch. In the first sketch the quick, jumpy, dark pattern expresses a feeling of excitement. In the second, the lights and darks express excitement in relation to the value of the background. If the background is light, the darks will be more emphatic; if dark, the lights will jump. In sketch Number 3, the light areas attract the eye. This sketch is interesting in relation to chiaroscuro painting. When this technique was first used, lights were contrasted against darks and darks against lights. But as painting became more sophisticated, various gradations of dark were allied, and the light pattern was emphasized against them. Many of the paintings of Andrea del Sarto, Raphael and Titian are interesting in this respect.

The fourth sketch indicates how the illusion of mystery is created as the bottle drifts in and out of the background. The shaded side of the bottle is lost in the shadow, the light side disappears into the light, and the transition tones are closely united with the background. Emphasis on the bottle is slight, just enough to suggest its character. Derivations of the same principle are indicated in the fifth and sixth sketches. In Number 5, the bottle is united with the background in a crisp, exciting way. In Number 6, emphasis is placed on the object. The edges are similar in value to the background, and thus subordinated, while the forward lights and darks are

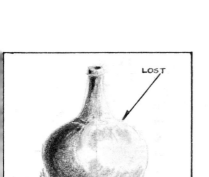

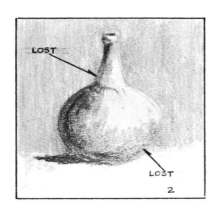

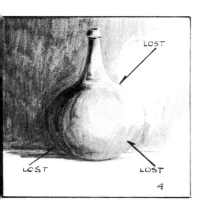

FIGURE 88. PRINCIPLES OF EMPHASIS AND SUBORDINATION.

145

FIGURE 89. ANGULAR FORMS AGAINST SOFT SKY.

emphasized. This brings the bottle into high relief. If one examines the dark portraits of Rembrandt and others of his school, he will see how skillfully and effectively this method of suggestion was employed. The way in which Rembrandt used the principle of emphasis and subordination has much to do with the mystery one feels in his paintings—both the portraits and landscapes. "The Old Mill" is a classic example among his landscapes.

If one wishes to suggest a line without emphasizing it, he might relate it to a similar line, for example a curve to a curve, or an angle to another angle. If emphasis is desired, play curves against angles or angles against curves. And so it is with form; an angular mountain against a softly fused sky (Figure 89) will be more emphatic than a curved edge against the same sky (Figure 90). The angular sharp saguaros in Figure 89 lend even more emphasis than the curved grasses in Figure 90. If the painter wants to create an illusion through the use of value, form should be subordinated by playing light against light and dark against dark. If the emphasis of form or pattern is desired, contrast light against dark, or vice versa.

The principles of emphasis and subordination also can be applied to hue and intensity. A warm object against a warm background will mysteriously drift into its

FIGURE 90. CURVED FORMS AGAINST SOFT SKY.

setting, while the same object against a cool background will stand out more distinctly. Similarly, the closer the value and intensity relation between the two, the less distinct the object will be. The greater the contrast, the more the object will stand out. A bright object against a dull background is more emphatic than a bright one against a bright background, or a dull object against a dull background. Again the closer the value and hue relation, the less distinct the object will be. When illusion is desired, similar hues and intensities are allied. When emphasis is required, opposites are used.

If value, hue and intensity are all involved, there is a good rule to remember—when hues are contrasted, keep values analogous, and when values are contrasted, keep hues analogous or play them against neutral, white or gray. The same result is achieved when a neutral is used in place of a hue.

The principle of subordination and emphasis can also be used in the juxtaposition of colors in small areas. Here one steps into the world of sophisticated painting. When one is able to key color—to place one color against another to increase or decrease emphasis, he has become a mature painter.

As an experiment in keying color cut a piece of white watercolor paper about

6 inches wide and 20 inches long. Divide it into 2½-inch squares and cut a 1-inch square opening in the center of each square, as illustrated in Figure 91. On the back of the sheet paste strips of colored paper of various hues across each set of squares so that the color showing in the two horizontal openings is identical. Neither the sequence nor the hues indicated in the diagram are important. If the color is subtle, however, the experiment will be more exciting. From here on one must write his own ticket. These suggestions will only furnish a clue. On the first set of squares (marked white in the diagram), paint the border in such a way that the left square appears lighter in value than the right. On the next set, the yellows, paint the border so that the left square looks brighter and lighter, and the right square darker and less intense. Place a scrap of the same yellow paper between the two squares and see if you have turned the trick. On the third set, the red, make the left square appear warm, and the right square cool. On Number four, the blue set, increase the intensity and lift the value on one square, lower the value and decrease the intensity on the other. Check with a piece of paper of the same blue. On the next, make one green square appear yellow-green and the other blue-green. On the orange set, bring out the red in one square and the yellow in the other; and on the last set raise the value of the violet and increase the blue in one, lower the value and bring out the red in the other. Check each set of squares with a piece of paper of the same color as you go along. These experiments can go on endlessly. The more you make the more you will know about keyed color.

Using the principle of subordination and emphasis, let us see if we can adequately interpret our feeling of the illusion and mystery surrounding a morning in early spring. Moisten the paper and allow yellow, yellow-green and violet to fuse lightly over the whole sheet. When the desired effect has been achieved, adjust the hue and value of the hills to the sky. As we come to the darks and graphic indications, we must exercise great restraint, for the significance of expression lies in suggestion, not explanation. The less said graphically, therefore, the better.

If one is an expressionist he should orient himself to his particular field of painting. Referring to the chart (Figure 78), he will find that he is in a middle position, with illustrative painting on one side and abstract on the other. Keeping a middle position between these two extremes calls for a good deal of balance. On the one hand, the expressionist must necessarily deal with nature and on the other hand, with perception. He must probe deeply into nature in a searching, analytical way in an attempt to broaden his understanding, and he must also delve into his own feelings. He is a thinking, feeling, acting person all wrapped up in the same bundle. The expressionist may lean toward story-telling, as Kipling or Oscar Wilde did in poetry, or he may prefer reducing the essential to a few lines, like the Oriental poets. Whether he leans one way or the other, his paintings should be poetic.

The expressionist is a person balanced between thinking and feeling. However, since the emphasis in life is usually on the thinking side, he must constantly devise ways of letting his perception dominate when he paints. Unless he does this, his thinking mind takes over and his expression is bound to become more analytical than poetic. One painter I know uses the device of talking to himself incessantly as he works, generally in a most disparaging way about everything. What he says has nothing to do with what he is painting. He can do the most highly suggestive

WHITE

YELLOW

RED

BLUE

GREEN

ORANGE

VIOLET

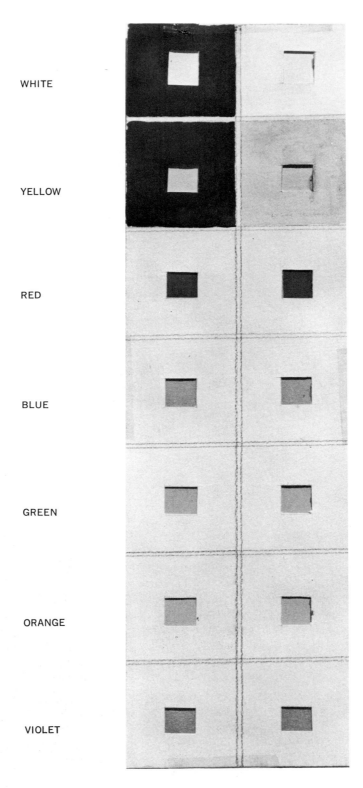

FIGURE 91. KEYED COLOR.

interpretation of Wyoming woodlands, and vehemently condemn everything in the state at the same time. And strange as it may seem, his paintings are always best when the mosquitoes are the worst.

There are many ways to suspend one's intellect before beginning to paint. One frequently used method is putting into words the emotion one feels in response to his subject. This is not easy. For example, if an artist sits down in front of a building he wants to paint, and decides to write something about it before he starts, he is apt to say only what his thinking mind tells him. In doing this, he is stuck with his own ideas. He is looking at himself, not the building. But suppose in his mind he turns over to his subject the words, "I am," and then sits back and lets the building talk to him. This is different. If he writes, "I am built of brick, I am solid, I am weathered, I am old," the building is speaking to him. Sooner or later he will feel the real substance of the emotion the building is giving him. Then he can express it through line, form, movement, shape and color.

Often music can help to quiet the mind. I do not mean interpreting music through painting, but allowing oneself to feel and be moved by its harmony and rhythm. In my school we often dance a bit while painting—not too actively, simply the swaying of one's shoulders or tapping of a toe. These methods are only suggestions; by experimenting you will doubtless be able to add a few of your own. When you realize that perception and feeling are just as important in painting as technical skill, the happy union is made. Only then is the artist on his way.

Chapter 13

ROUND-UP OF QUESTIONS

AND ANSWERS

Q. You discussed the use of the 1-inch brush in the early part of the book. Will you suggest other brushes that might be used?

A. The brushes illustrated in Figure 92 are those that I use most frequently, and with the exception of the 3-inch one, that I carry with me in the field. The 1-inch brush, an Art and Sign Golden Stroke No. 919, is not a pure red sable but a sabaline. It is less expensive than a sable and more desirable in that it has more snap. The 2-inch brush, a Delta No. 216, is a camel-hair brush that can usually be found in paint stores. It is a good water carrier but not well adapted to rough brushing or wiping out. When this brush is new, the hairs have a tendency to loosen. If a few become dislodged when you are painting, don't try to remove them when the paper is wet. Dust them off when the sheet dries. To stop the brush from shedding, soak it in water overnight, and if this is not effective, place it in a vise at the place where hairs and ferrule meet, and tighten gently. This must be done with care; if too much pressure is used, the hairs may divide. If it fails, get a new brush; they are not expensive. This brush is carried in the top of the mixing tray in the paint box. The 3-inch brush is similar to the Delta but the hairs are set more securely. It has no number or trade mark but is excellent to use on full sheets. The large pointed brush is a Fielding No. 12 red sable. Grumbacher makes a less expensive one. The smaller sable is a No. 6.

Q. What is the best way to select a brush?

A. A brush is a tool and should be selected for the work you expect it to perform. I never buy a brush without testing it in water, and any art store clerk will supply a cupful if you ask him to. Wash the brush thoroughly and get all the filler out. When the brush is fully charged, the thickness will indicate its water-carrying capacity. The resilience or snap may be determined by pushing the edge into the palm of the hand, or stroking the hairs over one's thumb. This should be done when the brush is wringing wet. By drawing the brush between finger and thumb and shaping it, one will see if it has a sharp edge. Requisites for a good brush are water-carrying capacity, resilience, and edge. Brushes vary however in any make, and price is not always the criterion. Round brushes may be tested in a similar manner, although one should not expect resilience in a soft-haired brush.

Q. How should one care for brushes?

A. Shape your brushes when you have finished painting and be sure they do not rest on their edges or points when they are carried. This is the advantage of having the brush holder in the watercolor box. Bent hairs in a brush may never straighten out. When brushes dry out the mass of hairs in the ferrule may loosen. This can often be corrected by soaking the brush overnight, or if this fails, putting the ferrule in a vise. If the brush begins to divide, straighten the hairs with a fine comb or brush, moisten it, shape it and let it dry. If this fails, repeat the process using a thin solution of honey. When storing your brushes, box them with crystals. Moths love red sable. If a brush has been used with India ink or tempera, wash it well in cold water before the ink or tempera dries. Never dip a watercolor brush in oil if you expect to use it again for watercolor.

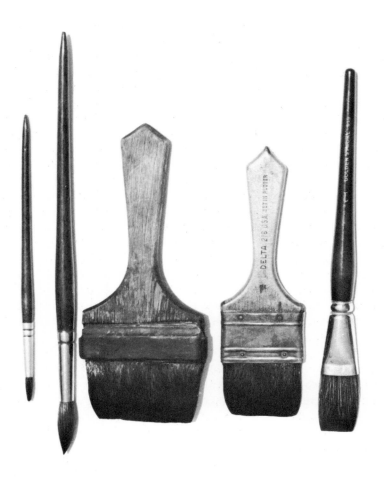

FIGURE 92. BRUSHES.

FIGURE 93. STRETCHING PAPER WITH TAPE.

Q. I have a difficult time stretching paper. Will you explain how to do it?

A. There are two customary ways: one with gummed tape and the other by stapling. We will consider the tape method first. Trim the deckle and cut the paper to a dynamic shape. If the paper is 140-pound weight or heavier, place it in a tub or tray of water and wash with a sponge to remove the surface film. If the paper is lighter weight, sponging will suffice. Soak 140-pound paper about three minutes; 300-pound paper takes five minutes or more, if it is unusually hard. Place the paper on a smooth, non-absorbent surface and sponge flat. Let the paper stand for about five minutes. This allows the water to thoroughly permeate the fiber and assures even expansion. Place the paper on the board. A balsa drawing board painted white is fine. Light pine, one half inch plywood or heavy, smooth masonite is usable. Heavy gummed tape 1 to 1½ inches wide is used. (Masking or Scotch tape will not work.) The tape is moistened by immersing quickly in a container of water. Do not use a brush or sponge as this takes off too much glue. The tape is stretched flat, with one-third of the width falling on the paper and two-thirds on the board. Stick the ends first to assure evenness. Press the tape to the paper and board with the fingers and then with an absorbent cloth such as an old towel. Do the opposite side and then the ends. After all four sides are secure, press the tape firmly down with the curved surface of a spoon or the flat of a knife handle. If the tape appears to be lifting, fasten it tightly with thumb tacks. Allow the paper to dry slowly in a horizontal position. If there are stretched sheets on both sides of the board, place it between two chairs to dry.

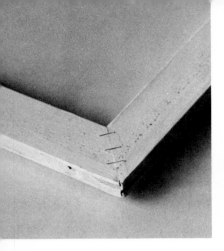

FIGURES 94-95. STAPLE METHOD OF STRETCHING PAPER.

The staple method is easier, faster and safer than the tape method. Trimming, soaking, sponging and waiting procedures are the same. Boards of balsa or pine may be used, but Plywood is difficult, Masonite impossible. I prefer canvas stretchers which are light and give a drum-like surface to work on when the paper is dry. Stretcher bars 23 by 16 are used for root two shapes, and 24 by 14 for root three. The ridge on the wooden pieces is planed off to afford a flat surface. The joints are glued together (Glue Bird will do) and stapled at each corner front and back (Figure 94). The stretcher is then painted white with water paint. Painting is repeated when the staple holes become too numerous, the paint serving as a filler and thus prolonging the life of the stretcher. I use a Swingline stapler, model 101, available at hardware stores, and size 101-5 staples. The extractor at the end of the device removes them easily. The stretcher fits the shade device perfectly (Figure 29), and the whole rig makes a light and efficient bit of field equipment.

In stretching the paper, set about five staples on one side of the paper and then five more on the opposite side and the same on either end. By stapling in a balanced way to the corners, one reduces the chance of wrinkles. Staples should be set about the width of the staple apart, as illustrated. The butt end of the stapler can be used to set the staples more securely when they are all placed.

Q. Are there ways of removing unsatisfactory painted areas in watercolor?

A. Yes. Natural, plastic or cosmetic sponges are handy for removing pigment in large areas, especially near the edges of the paper. Don't rub too hard. Try to loosen and lift the pigment rather than forcing it in. Dry with a tissue and apply water again. For small areas, a short fiber bristle brush or old toothbrush is good. Loosen the pigment and pick up with a tissue. A number of gentle applications of clean water is better than trying to do it all at once. Any of the kitchen scouring powders applied lightly with a stiff brush will bring paper back to white. To take out thin, white lines, use a ruling pen with water. Allow the water to stand till it practically disappears and pick up with a tissue. Apply a second and third time in the same way. A razor blade or sandpaper may be used on dry paper.

Q. Where was "Church Nocturne" painted?

A. In Marfil, near the city of Guanaguato, Mexico.

Q. How is it that sometimes one paints better than at other times—even better than he knows how?

A. I don't believe anyone paints better than he knows how. At one time he is probably thinking about how to do it and at another time he is not. Try thinking when you study and using your aware faculty when you paint.

Q. How do you keep pigments from hardening?

A. If you are painting regularly, lay a few strips of moistened tissues on the mixing tray of the box. I find a folded piece of "Miracloth" useful. This is also fine for cleaning the palette. If you are working on a studio palette, moisten a large natural sponge, or two or three synthetic ones and wrap the palette in a cellophane bag. The sponges hold the plastic away from the pigment. If you are folding up your equipment for a few weeks, lay strips of moistened tissues in the box and sprinkle with a few drops of Lysol to prevent molding. Fasten the box and wrap in a cellophane bag secured with a couple of heavy rubber bands. The same procedure may be used with the studio palette. To store tubes of pigment, place them in a tight jar with a bit of moistened sponge. If the sponge is too wet, the labels will come off. Pigments may be kept soft in this way for many months. Another satisfactory way is to box the pigments and store them in the refrigerator. It often happens that a pigment hardens on the surface in the watercolor box but remains soft underneath. This may occur when the palette is washed too frequently under the tap or when the pigment has become sun-baked outside. If it does, try turning the pigment over with a palette knife. The hard surface is lifeless but the under layer may be still fresh. Some painters soften hard pigment with a few drops of glycerine which I feel is a foolish economy. Once pigment has hardened, it loses its vitality. Softening it does not restore the luster. If you are economically minded and hesitate to dispose of hard pigment, estimate about how much it is worth and then compare its value with the piece of watercolor paper you are sure to ruin by using it. One of the surest ways to fail with watercolor is to paint with too little pigment or with hard pigment.

Q. Would you give us a few tips on painting water reflections?

A. Find a quiet pool and study it a while. You will see that all objects above water are sharper and more distinct than the reflections which are softly fused together. Many of the forms do not reflect, especially the low objects far back from the water's edge. The light hues are brighter above water than in the reflection and a bit lower in value. The darks however appear to lighten, sometimes mirroring the hue above, at other times simply darkening the value of the water. The pool seems motionless but then one notices that water is running in at one end and going out the other, and realizes that there must be some movement. Looking at the close side of the pool, the bottom can be seen. The sky is reflected near the center and the deep blue is a high sky reflection, for the pool is flat. It will be noted that the horizon line is not the water's edge, as it is at the ocean where sky and water meet, but is above the bank. It is another one of those planes that is looked down on.

What is the character of water? It certainly is wet. In this pool it is flat and gently moving. Possibly if these simple characteristics could be interpreted, it would be sufficient for a first attempt. There are a number of other things that are interesting—those reeds, that old snag, some floating weeds, a frog, a little fish, the pebbles on the bottom, a submerged log—to mention but a few. However, if the water is to be painted characteristically, some restraint must be exercised. The area above the water is painted first, the approach being one of divide and conquer. The water area is moistened, the sky reflection painted and allowed to dry. The area is moistened again, and the light hues above water that are reflected are pulled straight down and allowed to fuse. Now the darks are pulled down and allowed to fuse with the lights. If the transition is too sharp between lights and darks, the two are pulled together with the brush. At this stage, the water should begin to look wet. The moment the shine goes off the paper, the brush is thoroughly dried, and thin directional lines indicating the moving current are wiped out. If these lines are directed toward vanishing points, the water will lie flat. If the water appears too light in value when it dries, wet the area again and try a second time. If all is well, the painting, which actually deals with three foreground planes, is complete in two planes. However, it probably needs the indication of a close foreground area. A floating stick, half submerged log, grasses or a rock on the close bank might do. If anything in the water is used, it would be easier to employ the two previously established vanishing points.

Q. **How do you paint fast flowing water?**
A. When quiet water is considered expressively, we note that all the essentials necessary for the interpretation of a quiet emotion are presented to us by nature. Transitions are soft. Value, hue and intensity are analogous. Hue is subdued and generally in the quieter section of the wheel. The project is similar to the rainy day interpretation mentioned in Chapter 11 on Expression. All you have to do is to select with restraint. When you come to rushing water, however, the proposition is different, for such aspects in nature are exciting; while the water is rushing and turbulent, the lines are still curved, the transitions are soft, the values analogous, and the hues subdued. To express an exciting emotion, angularity and sharp contrasts of light and dark are mandatory, but to introduce such elements into the water would be to deny its character. Painting rushing

QUIET WATER

FAST WATER

water is an exciting, creative project, for you are dependent on what occurs in line, form, value, hue and intensity around the water, rather than in it. The water itself can be left practically untouched but if you use the proper expressive elements around the edge, it will really sparkle, rush and roar.

Q. Do you ever do watercolors in your studio from drawings made in the field?

A. Yes. When you do field drawings with the intent of working from them later inside, I would suggest that you use a broad medium. Avoid hard pencils, and draw in large masses rather than in a linear manner. Charcoal, Conti crayon or broad pencils are good. Sauce crayon and a tortillon or stub get massed effects quickly. Wash drawings and gray chalk drawings are good references.

Q. Do you ever paint on smooth board?

A. Yes. Rough paper is already a gray paper as each little bump casts a shadow and creates a gray tonality. Rough paper therefore can never reflect as much luminosity as a smooth surface. I prefer Strathmore heavy-duty regular surface. However, smooth paper or board presents difficulties and I would not recommend it until one is proficient on rough paper. Drying is rapid and spotty. Rough brushing is practically eliminated for textural indications. Fusing, which calls for split second timing, and lifting with a brush, are the techniques employed. Value progression from light to dark is practically out, for darks must be fused with the lights at the right moment. The light passages on smooth paper are not as difficult as the darks, for dark, hard edges stand out on smooth board like razor gashes. An interesting compromise between rough and smooth paper is made by sanding. If one wishes to interpret a sky in a more luminous way than would be possible on rough paper, the sky area can be sanded down. A package of assorted sand papers and a block will do the trick (Figure 96). The paper should be stretched on a board by the staple method, as tape is apt to be worn off. Paper can also be made rougher than it actually is by pounding it with an ice hammer or beating it with coarse sand paper or a flat grater. Both methods were used in painting the watercolor "Two Windmills" (page 53). It was done on a day when the sky was lusciously transparent and the ground looked unusually rough.

Q. You mentioned a watercolor procedure that involved applying pigment before the drawing was introduced. Are there others you could suggest?

A. Most watercolors call for different approaches. Sometimes a number are tried before the right one is discovered. If one feels that the impact of the subject depends more on form than color, an interesting way is to begin with form. Paint the whole subject with transparent black down to the last dark. The form will be revealed and the value pattern fixed in mind. Dry the paper thoroughly and wash it in a tray or under the tap with a soft sponge. The black pigment will stain only to value 2 to 2½. Darker values will wash off. Color may now be applied in a flowing manner or more selectively. The under gray will serve as a

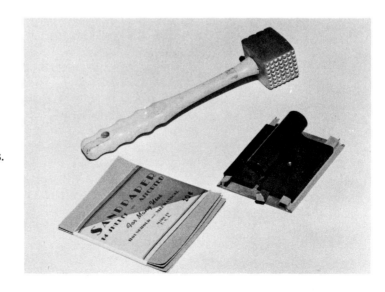

FIGURE 96. TEXTURE TOOLS.

unifying agent, and the hue will enliven the form. When using this approach, remember that large areas of paper should be left unpainted in the initial application of black, for as color is applied, the hue range will be limited, and intensity and light value balances will be called for. Unless white paper is available, this will not be possible. This procedure can be effective, used according to the principle of subordination and emphasis as illustrated in sketches 5 and 6 of Figure 88 (page 145).

It is often impractical to do a full sheet watercolor in the field, yet the subject may call for the spontaneity and freshness that only nature can supply. To compensate for the loss that must inevitably occur if the painting is done completely in the studio, it may be advisable to do the drawing in the field and even apply the first few washes. If one returns directly to the studio and finishes the painting, much of the spontaneity may be preserved.

An interesting approach with dark, mysterious subjects, is to work on wet paper. Trim the deckle of a heavy piece of paper and make a light, sketchy drawing in charcoal. Immerse the paper in a tray of water until it is thoroughly soaked (five minutes at least). Place it on a nonabsorbent surface, such as a large piece of Formica or a sheet of glass, and sponge it tight to the surface. This will make the surface semi-dry. Apply the light values in a general way all over the paper, letting them fuse together, using only transparent pigments. As the paper dries, merge down to darker values with your long-value-range, brilliant transparents. Avoid black and any of the long-range, low intensity transparents or earth colors. One will get sufficient neutralization as the dark brilliants combine. As the paper dries, go darker and darker, using the brush to lift and pull pigment together. When the paper has reached the stage where it is dry in some spots and semi-dry in others, dry the whole surface thoroughly. The watercolor should now be in a semi-amorphous state with the lights fairly bright and the darks drifting down below middle value. Little of an emphatic nature should yet be revealed. When you are sure the surface is dry, slide the paper back in the tray of water. You might think the pigment would lift but it will not, unless the water is agitated or a brush or sponge is applied. Soak the paper for a couple of minutes and carefully return it to the board. If water is applied to the nonabsorbent surface, the paper will lie flat and smooth. No sponging down, of course. The glistening wet painting is now in condition to be worked on all over. As the surface dries, the pigment is applied more and more heavily. The brush is used continuously to lift and add pigment on a wet surface. Copious quantities must be used. Remember, the water is on the paper. When the paper is dry, put in the final darks and linear suggestion. Lines will always be a bit soft for the paper is still wet under the surface. Watercolors done in this way are apt to buckle when they dry. To avoid this, dry them in a press. A drawing board and a weight will do. "Church Nocturne" shown on page 126 was done in this manner.